The Red Stockings of Cincinnati

The Red Stockings of Cincinnati

BASE BALL'S FIRST ALL–PROFESSIONAL
TEAM AND ITS HISTORIC
1869 AND 1870 SEASONS

by
Stephen D. Guschov

McFarland & Company, Inc., Publishers
Jefferson, North Carolina, and London

British Library Cataloguing-in-Publication data are available

Library of Congress Cataloguing-in-Publication Data

Guschov, Stephen D., 1965–
    The Red Stockings of Cincinnati : base ball's first all
–professional team and its historic 1869 and 1870 seasons / by
Stephen D. Guschov.
        p.   cm.
    Includes bibliographical references (p.   ) and index.
    ISBN 0-7864-0467-1 (sewn softcover : 50# alkaline paper) ∞
    1. Cincinnati Red Stockings (Baseball team)   I. Title.
GV875.C65G87   1998
796.357'64'0977178 — dc21   97-50027
                                                              CIP

Manufactured in the United States of America

McFarland & Company, Inc., Publishers
    Box 611, Jefferson, North Carolina 28640

Table of Contents

Preface

(Soon) every member of the first class nines of the country
will be a paid professional player, and hundreds of our
young men will aim at such a position as one of the most
shining pinnacles that fame can boast.

The *Paterson (N.J.) Press*, 1867

One of the most common complaints about baseball today is that it's a business and no longer a game. This is not an entirely accurate statement. Baseball has *always* been a business.

Since that first hazy afternoon in 1839 when Abner Doubleday hauled out a lopsided ball of cowhide and a crudely hewn stick of white ash (or so the myth goes), the game has always centered on money. The great Joe DiMaggio was a holdout with the New York Yankees early in his career, and when Joltin' Joe finally agreed to a contract he was booed by the Yankee Stadium fans for his alleged greediness. Boston Red Sox owner Harry Frazee sold Babe Ruth to the Yankees because Frazee didn't want to double the Bambino's salary from $10,000 to $20,000 in 1920. The biggest scandal in baseball history, the 1919 Black Sox scandal, occurred in part because Chicago club owner Charles Comiskey would not pay his players a postseason bonus that they had been expecting. The simple fact, as devoid of nostalgia and romance as it may be, is that the bottom line has always been the most important statistic in baseball.

In your hands is the story of the 1869–1870 Cincinnati Red Stockings — the first team in baseball history to pay all of its players a regular salary. The Red Stockings, under manager and captain Harry Wright, were pioneers in the game of professional baseball, and they had many of the same money problems that plague the game today. To borrow a line from Harry Truman: The buck started there.

"(Soon) every member of the first class nines of the country will be a paid professional player, and hundreds of our young men will aim at such a position as one of the most shining pinnacles that fame can boast."

The *Paterson Press*, 1867

"The leading Base Ball club of Cincinnati, seeing the inevitable ... threw down the gauntlet of defiance to the National Association of Base Ball Players — not by a flaming pronunciamento, but by manly declaration that henceforth it would be known as a professional organization."

Albert G. Spalding,
on the 1869 Cincinnati Red Stockings

1. Base Ball Before the Red Stockings

The 1869 Cincinnati Red Stockings were not the first baseball club in the game's history, nor were the Red Stockings the first team to employ professional players.

While the origins of the national pastime have been woven into a wonderfully mythical tapestry, it is ascertainable that as early as 1744, a reference to "base-ball" was contained in *A Little Pretty Pocket-Book*, which was published in London by John Newbery.[1] The first American account of the game occurred some thirty years later, when George Ewing, a Revolutionary War soldier, noted that he played in a game of "base" at Valley Forge, Pennsylvania, on April 7, 1778.[2] Perhaps George Washington was both the father of our country and the father of our national pastime.

In 1786, eight years after Ewing's journal account, a Princeton University student scratched the following entry into his diary: "A fine day, play 'baste ball' in the campus but am beaten for I miss both catching and striking the ball."[3] A year later, in 1787, Princeton banned the playing of ball games on the school grounds because such activity created "low and unbecoming gentlemen" and presented a "great danger to the health by sudden and alternate heats and colds and as it tends by accidents ... to disfiguring and maiming those who are engaged in it."[4]

As the nineteenth century dawned, youngsters frequently were seen playing "town-ball" or "round-ball" on village greens. The rules of the game varied from town to town, state to state, and region to region. In fact, some referred to the pastime as "the Massachusetts game" or "the New York game" in order to properly distinguish the many variations on the types of games played. The Massachusetts game, by way of example, featured an irregular four-sided field, with the batter (or "striker," as he originally was called) standing away from home plate. Outs in the Massachusetts game were made by either catching the ball on the fly or on one hop, or by "soaking" the runner with the ball.[5] The pastime became so popular that the city of Worcester prohibited ballplaying in its streets in 1816.[6] In Rochester, New York, in 1825, about fifty citizens began to play ball on a regular basis. The Rochester players ranged in age from eighteen to forty, and they met every afternoon during the summer to play the still-primitive sport on a small portion of a ten-

1

acre ground in the city.[7] By 1834, Robin Craver's *Book of Sports* observed that "base or 'goal ball'" rivaled cricket in popularity in the United States.[8]

By 1842, a group of New York City businessmen were playing ball, with eleven to a side, in a park on the corner of Twenty-Seventh Street and Fourth Avenue in downtown Manhattan, near where Madison Square Garden was later built. Among the Gotham amateurs was a twenty-two-year-old bank clerk named Alexander Joy Cartwright. On September 23, 1845, Cartwright organized the Knickerbockers, who were recognized as the first baseball club ever formed. The Knickerbockers adopted many of the same rules that exist today, including a diamond-shaped field, a ninety-foot distance between bases, foul territory, and three outs per side. The Knickerbockers, however, employed only eight men in the field: a "pitch," a "behind," three basemen, and three outfielders. And the "pitch" stood only forty-five feet away from home plate. The Knickerbockers, when not playing baseball, also sponsored club dinners, formal balls, and other Victorian-era social activities.

A rival squad known as the New York Club soon was established across town, and on June 19, 1846, the Knickerbockers met the New York Club on a cricket pitch in Hoboken, New Jersey, known as the Elysian Fields. The Knickerbockers had rented part of the pitch for use as a ball field, and would board the Barclay Street ferry every afternoon to ride over to New Jersey for their matches.

The New York Club featured several former cricketers, and they were far more adept at "striking"—or hitting—the ball than were the Knickerbockers. The New York Club trounced Cartwright's crew, 23–1, in what was believed to be the first true contest in the history of the game. Knickerbocker President Duncan F. Curry noted that the New York Club hurler "could pitch an awfully speedy ball" that served to handcuff his squad of strikers.[9] Alexander Cartwright umpired the historic tilt, and established immediate arbitral authority by fining James Whyte Davis for swearing during the contest.[10] After the game, according to the terms of the challenge, the Knickerbockers had to buy the New York Club dinner, and the two teams adjourned to the nearby McCarty's Hotel for their hardball repast.

Interest in the new sport flourished in the late 1840s. New clubs, including the New York Gothams, the Brooklyn Eagles, and the Philadelphia Olympics, were established. The shortstop position was added during the same time period. By 1849, the Knickerbockers were sporting the first baseball uniforms, featuring a white flannel shirt, long, blue woolen trousers, and a straw hat.[11] In the same year, Alexander Cartwright ventured west to take part in the California gold rush. It took the Knickerbocker founder 156 days to travel from Newark to San Francisco, but at every stop Cartwright dug out a weathered ball and bat and introduced the game of baseball to settlers along the way.[12]

Companies and towns began forming their own teams in the1850s. It was not uncommon for a prospective employee to be asked about his hardball skills when he applied for a job in those days.

In 1858, the National Association of Base Ball Players was formed. The association initially consisted of approximately fifty teams in the eastern and midwestern United States, and also included some university clubs. No southern ball clubs joined the NABBP at its outset due to the regional hostilities that were about to explode into the Civil War.[13] The NABBP was organized to set standard rules and regulations, and to keep the game amateur and gentlemanly. Professional players were banned from the association, as were players deemed to be of low social standing. The NABBP desired to make "base ball" (Note: *baseball* did not come to be used exclusively as a single word until early in the twentieth century) a sport strictly for society's elite class. Even within the NABBP, some clubs would not play others deemed socially inferior in class.

Among the playing rules adopted by the NABBP were many that gave the strikers a decided advantage. Pitchers threw underhanded, and they stood forty-five feet away from home plate. The striker could use any size bat whatsoever, and was under no obligation even to swing at pitches that were right down the middle of the plate. An umpire would call a strike only if the striker repeatedly passed up such well placed fare.[14]

The *New York Clipper*, a popular journal of the era, noted in 1860 how baseball by that point had surpassed cricket in popularity because "in the one case the spectators could enjoy a quickly played and exciting contest, marked by beautiful fielding, and in the other they had to wait hours, and visit the grounds two days, to see isolated instances of good play in fielding — skill in batting, except that shown by free hitting, not being appreciated by the generality of those who visit cricket and base ball grounds."[15]

The event that played the biggest role in popularizing baseball across America was the Civil War. Union soldiers, in particular, played baseball to relax and relieve some of the stress of combat. Even in Confederate prison camps, captive soldiers would group together and start up a game, often introducing the sport to their captors for the very first time. On Christmas Day, 1862, two squads made up of soldiers from the 165th New York Volunteer Infantry staged a game at Hilton Head, South Carolina, which was witnessed by approximately 40,000 men.[16] The crowd probably was the largest ever to see a sporting event in the United States up to that date.[17] Thousands of soldiers wrote letters home and made diary entries telling of the new-fangled sport to which they had been introduced. At war's end, soldiers took the game back home with them and taught it to their fellow townsfolk. Baseball was, for the most part, a unifying force after the Civil War, as the nation began to recover from its self-inflicted wounds.

2. Professionalism Enters the Game

It was during the years just prior to the Civil War that professionalism entered the game of baseball.

The first admission charge occurred in 1858 when 1,500 fans, or "cranks," as they were then known, paid fifty cents admission to watch a New York vs. Brooklyn all-star series played at the Fashion Race Course grounds on Long Island.[1] The New York stars were led by future Red Stocking manager Harry Wright, and they bested the Brooklyn stalwarts two games to one.

A year after the 1858 all-star series, the *New York Clipper* reported a match between the Excelsior Club of Upton, Massachusetts, and the Union Club of Medway, Massachusetts, wherein the victorious squad received $500.[2] In 1860 the same two clubs would joust for a $1,000 prize.[3]

The first regular admission charges occurred in 1862. William H. Cammeyer of Brooklyn drained a winter skating pond that he owned, and he approached the New York Mutuals club with an offer to let them build a ballfield on the site. An agreement was reached wherein the Mutuals would use the premises, named the Union Grounds, on a rent-free basis, and Cammeyer would charge spectators ten cents each to watch a game.[4] Cammeyer and the Mutuals would then split the gate proceeds. The idea proved to be a profitable one. Two years later in 1864 the Brooklyn Atlantics fenced in their park, known as the Capitoline Grounds, and likewise began to charge a regular admission fee.[5]

The whole concept of charging an admission fee was controversial. Many people, particularly during the economically debilitating Civil War years, could not afford to pay to watch a ballgame. As a result, baseball continued to be a game primarily played for the enjoyment of society's elite class. The poorer members of society who desired to view a game, however, would try to get a vantage point on a contest by watching it from the top of a nearby tree or building if they could not afford to pay to get inside the ballpark.

Many people, however, applauded the idea of an admission charge as a means of keeping society's undesirables out of the ballpark. Henry Chadwick, who invented the scorebook and the box score system and was one of the founding fathers of the game, opined in the *Ball Players' Chronicle* that admission fees were "not relished by the masses, but by the respectable portion of the community it is regarded as a desirable improvement, as by means of the increased price hundreds of blackguard boys and roughs generally are kept out, while the respectable patrons of the game are afforded better opportunities for enjoying a contest."[6] Chadwick also condemned "the blasphemy and obscenity of the language used by the hooting assemblage which congregate on the outside and peep through the fence holes at the players."[7] The *Philadelphia Sunday Mercury* editorialized in favor of building an enclosed park in that metropolis so that "the visitor will not be annoyed by the gratuitous slang of the mob who generally congregate on important matches, and whose phraseology does not grate pleasantly upon polite ears."[8]

At the same time that admission charges first became part of the game, so did the practice of paying players.

While the NABBP forbade professional players from its member clubs, this rule was widely ignored and the association, which had little enforcement power, did virtually nothing to prevent the practice from occurring. The NABBP defined a professional as any player given "place or emolument."

The first professional baseball player was pitcher James P. Creighton of the Brooklyn Excelsiors in 1860. Creighton was paid, not unexpectedly, under the table by the Excelsiors in order to skirt the NABBP's regulations. Creighton met an early and tragic demise, however, when he ruptured his bladder while batting in a game against the Morrisania Unions on October 14, 1962. He died four days later at age twenty-one.

Alfred James Reach — the founder of the sporting good company of the same name — was probably the second paid player in the game. Reach's tactic was to hold himself out, free agent-style, to the highest bidder for his hardball talents. In 1864, Reach created quite a stir in the game by jumping from the New York Eckfords to the Philadelphia Athletics when the latter offered him the princely sum of $1,000 a season to play second base for them.

Clubs were varied and creative in the manner by which they paid their professional players. Some stars, like James Creighton, were paid under the table, while other players were given a share of the gate receipts, also in disregard of NABBP rules. Some players were given no-show jobs to perform, with the understanding and agreement that they really were being remunerated for their work on the ballfield and nothing more. One example of such a situation involved Albert G. Spalding, the legendary pitcher in the game's earliest days. Spalding noted that while he was hurling for the Forest City club of Rockford, Illinois, in 1867, he was approached by a Chicago citizen who offered him a job in a wholesale grocery in the Windy City for forty dollars a week "with the understanding that my store duties would be nominal, a chance given to play ball frequently, without affecting my salary to reduce it."[9]

In addition to being paid to perform no real work beyond their ballplaying duties, star players also received an abundance of free meals, drinks, clothing, and other services from local merchants grateful that they were toiling for the local nine. It reached the point where any baseball star literally would have no real expenses to meet. Everything was handed to him by members of the local business community who were happy to see him playing for the home team.

Another means of paying a player was to hold an all-star contest or benefit game in his honor, with a portion of the gate proceeds going to the player. Harry Wright, who would become the manager, captain, and starting center fielder for the 1869 Cincinnati Red Stockings, was feted at such a benefit in 1863 when he played for the Knickerbockers. Cranks were charged twenty-five cents to attend Wright's benefit game. For an additional quarter, the crank would receive a souvenir ticket from the benefit "with a picture of a Professional on each." Harry Wright reaped a total of $29.65 that afternoon.[10]

Perhaps the most common means by which a player would be paid to play baseball was to stick him in a questionable or nonexistent government job, particularly at the municipal and federal levels. George Wright, brother of Harry Wright and shortstop extraordinaire on the 1869 Red Stockings, was a member of the Washington Nationals club in 1867. Each of the Nationals allegedly was employed by the federal government, and that season's team roster listed each National player's civil service job along with his playing position. George Wright was listed as a government clerk, and his business address was given as 238 Pennsylvania Avenue in Washington. At that address on Pennsylvania Avenue, however, was nothing but a public park.[11] And, according to witnesses of the day, one was more likely to find George Wright playing ball on the "White lot" across from the White House, as opposed to clerking for Uncle Sam, during what were supposed to be his normal working hours. *Washington Evening Star* writer Thomas Henry commented on this charade by labeling the U.S. Treasury Department "the real birthplace of baseball."[12]

The most egregious example of such sinecurism was in New York City. The notorious Gotham politico, William Marcy "Boss" Tweed, owned the New York Mutuals club there. Tweed stashed several of his players on the city payroll, where they allegedly toiled as clerks, sweepers, and street cleaners. One of Boss Tweed's officers on the Mutual BBC was New York City Coroner John Wildey, and the City Coroner's office also became a hardball haven for many of Tweed's Mutual players. Perhaps this type of arrangement was perfectly reasonable, given that it was happening just prior to the game's "deal-ball" era. Regardless, it was estimated that Boss Tweed cost New York City taxpayers some $30,000 a year in phony salaries being doled out to his Mutual players.[13]

Not every player on a team was paid, of course — only the stars — but with each passing season, more and more players received some sort of remuneration. Henry Chadwick estimated, by way of example, that by 1868 ten members of the Brooklyn Eckfords were professionals in one manner or another.

As money entered into the game to a greater and greater extent, so did problems related to gambling, bribery, and corruption.

Crookedness began to run rampant as many players sought to make more money on the side by either throwing games outright or at least rigging the outcome or the number of runs scored. This practice of throwing or rigging a contest was known as "hippodroming." The existence of admission fees contributed to the hippodroming problem by virtue of the fact that often when two clubs played a three-game series, they would agree beforehand to split the first two games, so as to build up the excitement level and ticket demand for the third game, and thus guaranteeing that lucrative gate receipts would be shared by the two clubs. Eventually, however, the paying public caught on to this sham, and if there was any inkling by the cranks that the fix was in, then the two suspected ball clubs would be playing before the groundskeepers and nobody else. When the Washington Nationals posted a sign in 1867 that read "BETTING POSITIVELY PROHIBITED," it was meant as much for the Washington players as it was for the fans in the stands.

The NABBP lacked the power, will, and courage to do anything about the problem, but all the while promoted the guise that all of its member clubs were strictly amateur in nature. Open betting became commonplace inside ballparks, and it was not uncommon to see known gamblers openly consorting with ballplayers before and even during games.

Not unexpectedly, the first players to be disciplined by the NABBP for accepting bribes were a couple of Boss Tweed's boys, William Wansley and Ed Duffy, after Tweed's powerhouse Mutuals threw a game against the Brooklyn Eckfords on September 28, 1865.[14] Wansley and Duffy induced their teammate Thomas Devyr to join them in the unsavory scheme, and paid him $300 for his role in it. The NABBP, however, only saw fit to briefly suspend the guilty players, and all three later returned to the crooked Tweed club. *Harper's Weekly* weighed in that "so common has betting become that the most respectable clubs in the country indulge in it to a highly culpable degree, and so common ... the tricks by which games have been 'sold' for the benefit of gamblers that the most respectable participants have been suspected of baseness."[15] Some political observers of the day felt that the rising level of corruption in the game of baseball in the middle to late 1860s mirrored that in the scandal-plagued administration of President Andrew Johnson.

Another major problem in the game in the pre–Red Stocking era was that of "revolving," wherein a player would breach his agreement with a club and jump to another team that offered him more money, or at least a higher-paying phantom job. It was an avid seller's market for ballplayers in the 1860s, and once again a situation existed wherein the NABBP did little to enforce its own rules prohibiting such conduct. The NABBP regulations stipulated that a player could not play for multiple clubs at the same time, and a player had to wait for thirty days after he left a club before he could start playing for another one. These NABBP rules, however, were rarely enforced.

An early example of this sort of problem involved one of the future Red Stocking stars. George Wright, one of the standouts of the game in the 1860s, played for the New York Gothams in a victory over Newburg's Hudson City club while he also was a member of the Philadelphia Olympics ball club.[16] Wright tried to avoid suspicion by using the surname "Cohen" when he toiled for the Gothams, but his secret got out. The *Philadelphia Sunday Mercury* editorialized that its city's ball clubs should pursue "native amateur talent rather than professional players from rival cities, who cannot be expected to have the welfare of the club at heart as much as our own men ... revolving players go in a gambling spirit for what they can get, caring little for the higher attributes of the ball player."[17] Harry Wright, future manager of the Red Stockings, weighed in that "any player violating a legal contract by signing a second contract with another club ... should be expelled from the Association."[18] This banishment, of course, would have spelled trouble for Harry's older brother George, he of the "Wright"/"Cohen" mutable monikers.

It was against this backdrop that an interest soon developed with respect to the establishment of an openly, all-professional baseball club. Such a club, its advocates declared, could attract top-playing talent at top-dollar salaries, and in doing so would not be as likely to fall prey to problems associated with gambling, hippodroming, and revolving. And, most importantly, it was believed that baseball cranks would line up in droves — dollar-waving droves — to see such a superior hardball product.

3. A Quest in the Queen City

Admirers of the city of Cincinnati called it the "Queen City of the West," while detractors referred to it as "Porkopolis," a slur against its reputation as a leading city in the hog industry. The citizens of Cincinnati wanted a desirable national identity; something that would put an end to the "Porkopolis" taunt. Cincinnatians saw a baseball club as the perfect answer.

On July 23, 1866, twenty-six-year-old Aaron B. Champion established a new amateur baseball club in Cincinnati. Baseball had been played in the Queen City since at least 1860, and by the end of the Civil War two clubs already had been established there: the Buckeye Base Ball Club and the Live Oak Base Ball Club.

Champion was a lawyer with the Cincinnati firm of Tilden, Sherman & Moulton. He was not much of a ballplayer himself, but Champion was an enormous civic booster. He believed that if the city of Cincinnati prospered, so would he. Thus, he sought to promote the burg via his new Cincinnati Base Ball Club, a squad that he hoped would be able to compete with the best teams in the land.[1]

Indeed, a club is precisely what Champion formed in 1866, although not in quite the same context as it would be thought of today. Rather, what Champion established with his fellow barristers was a club in the more ordinary sense of the word, akin to a country club in the present age, together with membership requirements and a constitution and by-laws. There were seventeen original members in Champion's club. Members would pay dues to join, but only a few of the men would actually play the game of baseball.

The club was as much social in nature as it was sporting. When one was accepted as a member of the Cincinnati Base Ball Club, he received a letter that read: "[At] a meeting of the Cincinnati Base Ball Club held [date inserted here] you were duly elected an active member thereof. Enclosed you will please find statement of Club charges for ensuing year. By calling upon the Treasurer and paying same you will receive member's ticket."[2]

Aaron Champion was elected president of the newly formed club. Other officers included iron merchant Thomas G. Smith as vice president, insurance company executive Edward E. Townley as treasurer, and businessman John P. Joyce as club secretary.[3]

In 1866, the club's first year of existence, it played its home games at the Live Oak Base Ball Grounds, paying $2,000 for the use of the field for the season. The Cincinnati Base Ball Club adopted the name "Red Stockings" and posted a record of two wins and two losses in its inaugural campaign. The Cincinnati Base Ball Club played three of its four games that year against its newly adopted crosstown rivals, the Buckeyes, who handed the Red Stockings both of their defeats in the 1866 season.

A year later the club leased the grounds of the Union Cricket Club for its home tilts. Most club members referred to the field as the Union Grounds, although it also was known as the Union Cricket Club Grounds and the Lincoln Park Grounds, given the fact that the eight-acre, fenced grounds were located in a small park behind Lincoln Park in Cincinnati, near the Union Terminal.[4] It was a twenty-minute ride by streetcar to the Union Grounds from the heart of downtown Cincinnati.

Aaron Champion ordered that approximately $10,000 worth of improvements be made to the home grounds for the 1867 season, including grading and sodding of the field and building of a new clubhouse and stands.[5] The Union Cricket Club was a membership-oriented organization similar to the Cincinnati Base Ball Club. Many of the Union Cricket Club members and players became fascinated by the new sport they were watching, and soon membership in the cricket club dwindled and membership in the baseball club flourished. By 1867, Champion's club would count 380 members on its rolls.[6] There was a certain member of the Union cricket professionals who also had played a fair amount of baseball in his youth, and one afternoon he approached Aaron Champion about the possibility of joining the Red Stocking club. That cricket player's name was Harry Wright.

William Henry "Harry" Wright was born in Sheffield, England, on January 10, 1835. As a young boy he emigrated to America with his family. His father, Samuel Wright, was a noted cricket player in England, and Samuel had come to the United States to work as a cricket pro at the St. George Cricket Club on Staten Island, New York. Two more sons, George and Samuel Jr., were added to the Wright family after they started their new life in America.

All three Wright sons were natural athletes, and all three excelled at cricket. Harry called the sport his first love. He was less enamored of school, however, and dropped out at age fourteen to work for a jewelry manufacturer.

A few years later, Harry left the gem world and signed on as a professional cricketer for twelve dollars a week with the St. George Dragonslayers — the crew coached by his father, Samuel. The club soon relocated to Hoboken, New Jersey, and when Harry was not out on the cricket field defending his wicket, he would journey over to the adjacent Elysian Fields and watch Alexander Cartwright's Knickerbockers have at this new sport of "base ball."

The new game became a source of fascination to Harry. There were definite similarities to his native sport of cricket: in both games, one batted a ball, ran to a base, and scored runs. The arbitrators in both sports were called umpires. At the same time, however, baseball and cricket were quite different. A cricket game could go on for days, while a baseball contest lasted only a couple of hours. In cricket a player never was to question the decision of the umpire. In baseball, though, a player might spit tobacco on the umpire's shoes and threaten to toss him into the Hudson River if he did not like a call. Soon, Harry Wright began to devote more and more of his spare time to learning about and playing the new sport.

In 1858, Harry joined the Knickerbockers as a player. He played short-stop and outfield for the club, and in his first game, on July 8, 1858, he scored three runs and made three fine catches in a 31–13 loss to the Brooklyn Excelsiors at the Fashion Race Course Grounds on Long Island.[7]

Harry Wright threw and batted from the right-handed side. He stood 5 feet 9½ inches and tipped the scales at a wiry 157 pounds. He cut a hirsute appearance with his mustache, goatee, and sideburns. He wore round spectacles. An associate described Harry as "tall, good-looking, neatly dressed, somewhat clerical in appearance."[8] Another friend called him "a strong, muscular athlete in full prime."[9] He spoke with a soft British accent, a remnant of his birthplace. He eschewed all use of alcohol, tobacco, and profanity.

From 1858 to 1864, Harry toiled for the Knickerbockers and became one of their star players. Harry was, of course, considered an amateur player, although he did have the famous 1863 "benefit" wherein he netted $29.65 in tribute. He continued to earn a legitimate living as a cricket professional in the New York and New Jersey area. His duties included giving lessons to club members, arranging matches, and promoting interest in the sport, much like a tennis pro or a golf pro might do today at a club. Harry Wright did not fight in the Civil War, and neither did either of his two brothers.

In 1865, Harry ventured westward from New York to Cincinnati to organize the Union Cricket Club, for which he was paid $1,200 annually. While in the Queen City, he discovered that baseball clearly had surpassed cricket in popularity. To Harry this also meant that baseball was becoming a more profitable venture than cricket. Cricket's appeal, Harry reasoned, was strictly limited to the elite in society, whereas baseball, despite a certain form of elitism found in admission charges back then, nonetheless had a broader appeal to the public as a whole, regardless of social stratum.

In 1866, Harry met Aaron Champion for the first time. They struck up an immediate friendship and, just as had happened when he first saw the Knickerbockers play several years prior, Harry began to focus more on a future in baseball and less on a future in cricket.

Aaron Champion knew of Harry Wright's success with the Knickerbockers, and in 1867 he offered Harry a spot with the Red Stockings. Harry signed on enthusiastically. He joined a Cincinnati club that featured other standout players such as pitcher/second baseman Asa Brainard, first baseman Charlie Gould, and third baseman Fred Waterman. The 1867 Cincinnati Red Stockings were an excellent ball club, and finished the campaign with a record of 17-1. The highlight of the season came on September 12 in a contest against the Holt Base Ball Club in Newport, Kentucky. The Red Stockings pummeled the Holt BBC by the eye-popping score of 109–15. The Red Stockings belted thirty-one home runs in the massacre, and star center fielder Harry Wright clouted seven roundtrippers himself in the drubbing.

Another memorable moment in the 1867 season occurred after a victory in Louisville. The Red Stockings decided to have a banquet on board the boat on which they were traveling, in celebration of their win. The ship's captain, however, noticed that there were numerous female passengers on board and feared that things could get a little out of hand, given the highly combustible combination of rowdy and randy baseball players, wine, women and song — and all happening out on the Ohio River. As Cincinnati baseball writer Harry Ellard described it:

> The mind of the captain was very much exercised lest the exhuberant spirits of the victors would disturb his fair passengers, and he made the request that there should be no undue noise or hilarity. With gentlemanly sense of honor, the victorious Red Stockings promised faithfully that the strictest decorum should be observed. This banquet stands on record as being the most unique, as well as the most silent one ever celebrated. Voices modulated to the lowest tone when toasts were proposed, no clinking glasses gave forth a sound, while "Hip, hip, hurrah!" was uttered in the most quiet manner. Champagne flowed freely, but the remarkable repression of ebullition of feeling among the Red Stockings seemed to temper the effect. The captain afterwards made the remark that it was the stillest party he ever saw, where so much wine was present.[10]

While the 109–15 vaporization of the Holt BBC and the later victory celebration on the Ohio River after a Louisville victory may have been the best moments of the Red Stockings' 1867 season, they were not the times on which the club focused over the winter of 1867-68. Rather, the Red Stockings brooded over the single blemish on their otherwise sterling record, a 53–10 beating on July 15 at the hands of the Washington Nationals. One Cincinnati baseball writer referred to the thrashing as "a Waterloo defeat."

What made the loss to Washington particularly galling to Harry Wright was that the star shortstop for the Nationals was none other than Harry's younger brother, George, who took fiendish delight in whipping his older brother's club. The Red Stockings knew that when they trounced the Holt BBC 109–15, they were beating up on a clearly outmatched nine. The

Washington Nationals, however, were one of the top clubs in the country, and the Red Stockings were striving to be competitive with such powerhouse teams. In losing to Washington as badly as they did, the Red Stockings knew that they needed to improve markedly. The Red Stockings — and the city of Cincinnati — were determined to have a top-shelf, nationally renowned hardball squad, and Aaron Champion was ready to empty his wallet if need be to do so.

4. Building a Ball Club

The first move that Aaron Champion made over the winter of 1867-68 was to name Harry Wright as the manager of the Red Stockings. Champion was committed to sculpting the Red Stockings into world-beaters, and he realized that it was going to cost money to do so. All of the best clubs in the game, such as the Philadelphia Athletics, Washington Nationals, and Brooklyn Atlantics, were paying top dollar, albeit under the table, for the game's premium talent, and so Champion ordered Wright to go out and sign players of similar caliber. Champion was ready to send Harry Wright all the way back to Sheffield, England, if necessary, in order to recruit such hardball talent.

In order to pay for the players, Aaron Champion decided to charge ten cents admission for the Red Stockings' home games at the Union Grounds in Cincinnati.[1] Additionally, Champion successfully lobbied the club's directors for approval of an $11,000 stock issue to be used to refurbish the ballfield, make improvements on the fenced-in grounds, and equip his nine.[2] Stock subscribers were enticed with an offer of free admission to the Union Grounds during the baseball and winter skating seasons. The stock issue, however, was not a huge success, raising only $3,000 which went to make the necessary improvements at the Union Grounds and also pay down a note made by Champion on behalf of the club.[3]

It mattered little to Champion or Wright that they were skirting the NABBP rules by signing professional players. Everyone was doing it, and it was the only way to stay competitive.

Harry Wright's recruitment efforts resulted in a solid nucleus for the 1868 Red Stockings. In addition to Wright and 1867 holdovers Brainard, Gould, and Waterman, the 1868 Cincinnati nine featured such standouts as catcher John Hatfield and outfielders Moses Grant and Rufus King — a firm base that could match up against the iron of the hardball world.

Harry Wright was the perfect leader for this club. The *Cincinnati Enquirer* stated that he was a "baseball Edison. He eats base-ball, breathes base-ball, thinks base-ball, dreams base-ball, and incorporates base-ball in his prayers."[4]

In an era when ballplayers generally were a rowdy, carousing, boozing lot, Wright instilled a sense of discipline and regimen into his flannel-clad

The 1868 Red Stockings, who went 41-7 and featured Harry Wright (seated at the far left), F. Waterman (seated second from left), Charlie Gould (seated second from right), and Asa Brainard (standing on the far left) (NATIONAL BASEBALL LIBRARY, COOPERSTOWN, N.Y.).

troops. Wright stressed strong physical conditioning for his players and ordered regular sessions for practice and drills, particularly those related to cutoffs, relays, and defensive alignment. Wright also initiated a preseason, spring training-style warm-up program for his men. According to a letter by Wright, his club would

> receive orders to be at the Gymnasium for exercise from 10 to 12 A.M. [sic] and 2:30 to 4 P.M. This will consist of throwing, pitching, and catching, running and jumping, swinging light clubs and dumb bells, rowing, pulling light weights, and in fact doing a little of everything to keep them going and assist in making them supple and active. When the weather is favorable they will meet on the grounds in the afternoon at 2:30 for practice. This will comprise a half-hour's indiscriminate throwing, batting and catching; then they will assume their regular positions in the field, with, say two, taking alternate turns at batting — 8 strikes each, all hits counting — to be relieved by two others in turn until all have been at the bat. With three men at the bat, the bases can be run as in a game, giving two or three outs to each batsman. No loafing

or shirking should be permitted, and yet the Manager or Captain must study the temperaments of his men and be guided accordingly from commencement to end, in his judgment as to what should and should not be done. To preserve harmony in a nine, it is essential there should be no "chafing" or fault-finding with or by the players.[5]

In other letters detailing his squad's preseason regimen, Wright noted that his men would play handball.[6] Also, to instill a competitive edge in his nine, Wright on occasion would "excite a rivalry (in the afternoon batting practice) by keeping a record of the base hits."[7]

During games, it was not uncommon for Wright to be the only Red Stocking who spoke. He would bark instructions, move players around, and call to his fellow fielders as to who should catch a pop fly and who should stay nearby in case the ball was bobbled or dropped. Harry also used intricate hand signals to communicate with his strikers and baserunners — a first in the game.

Wright was quiet, honorable, and highly respected by his players. The *New York Clipper* noted that Harry was "unapproachable in his good generalship and management," and Henry Chadwick added that Wright's Red Stockings were "better trained and more practiced."[8] Wright once commented to an associate that he wanted his club to work together "like a nicely adjusted machine." Frequently he would cry out, "You need a little more ginger!" in order to light a fire under his team.[9] When Wright himself became excited, he would yell, "Sit still, my heart, sit still!" Harry Wright frequently referred to his club as "the boys," in a loving and paternal fashion, although it also was a fact that Wright was older than the rest of his mates by some ten to twelve years.[10]

Manager Wright indeed did ignite the 1868 Cincinnati Red Stockings, for they won forty-one out of the forty-eight games they played that season.

One of the Red Stockings' losses that season was to George Wright's Morrisania Unions club, which of course galled Harry Wright to no end. Another of the Cincinnati nine's defeats in 1868 occurred in a contest at the Union Grounds when a local umpire, seeking to win a favor with the Red Stockings, made a clearly erroneous call against a player on the opposing team. Harry Wright took it upon himself to overrule the overzealous umpire's call and rule against his own club. It wound up costing the Red Stockings the game, but it was a tribute to the character of Harry Wright, who would rather lose a game than win it by underhanded means.[11]

The highlight of the 1868 season for the Red Stockings was the club's pair of victories over its local rivals, the Buckeyes, 28–10 and 20–12. The two teams were vying for Queen City bragging rights. After the Buckeyes lost the first contest to the Red Stockings, they signed three Washington players for the rematch, although it made no difference to the final outcome. The Buckeyes were considered a skulduggerous lot who, according to the *Spirit*, a local periodical, were "ignoring all rules ... and even went so far ... as to drug some of the players of the Cincinnati Club and to bribe others."[12]

While the Red Stockings were successful on the field in 1868, the color red also shone brightly on the club's ledger books. The team ended the season with a deficit of $6,000. Aaron Champion, spurred by Cincinnati's 41-7 record, petitioned the board of directors for an additional $15,000 stock issue so that the Red Stockings could sign (and re-sign) players, renovate the Union Grounds, and purchase new equipment. The board complied, largely due to the fact that the Union Cricket Club had folded and had deeded to the Red Stockings all right, title, and interest to the Union Grounds, with the provision that the ball club assume all indebtedness — to the tune of approximately $7,500, as it turned out — and allow the cricketers to use the grounds for an occasional practice session. This arrangement was fine with the board, which had planned to raise additional funds anyway by flooding the Union Grounds over the winter and making use of it as a skating rink for club members.[13]

Harry Wright was married toward the end of the 1868 season to the former Carrie Mulford, and the club showed its appreciation and affection for its manager by giving him a gold watch, around which was wrapped a $100 United States government bond and a gold medal inscribed with the names of Wright and all the rest of the 1868 Red Stockings.[14]

The city of Cincinnati had grown enamored of its Red Stockings, and one of the club members was even inspired to memorialize the nine in verse:

THE CINCINNATI BASEBALL CLUB SONG.

BY A MEMBER.

(AIR — "BONNIE BLUE FLAG.")

We are a band of baseball players
    From "Cincinnati City;"
We come to toss the ball around,
    And sing to you our ditty.
And if you listen to our song
    We are about to sing,
We'll tell you all about baseball
    And make the welkin ring.

CHORUS.
Hurrah! Hurrah!
    For the noble game, hurrah!
"Red Stockings" all will toss the ball,
    And shout our loud hurrah.

Our Captain is a goodly man,
   And Harry is his name;
Whate'er he does, 'tis always "Wright,"
   So says the voice of fame.
And as the Pitcher of our nine,
   We think he can't be beat;
In many a fight, old Harry Wright
   Has saved us from defeat.

CHORUS.

The man who catches Harry's balls,
   It passes all belief,
He's so expert in catching "fouls"
   We have dubbed him "chicken thief."
And if a player's on his first,
   He'd better hold it fast;
With "Johnny Hat" behind the bat,
   The balls are seldom passed.

CHORUS.

In many a game that we have played,
   We've needed a First Base,
But now our opponents will find
   The "basket" in its place.
And if you think he "muffs" the balls,
   Sent into him red hot,
You'll soon be fooled by "Charlie Gould,"
   And find he "muffs" them not.

CHORUS.

We travel on to Second Base,
   And Brainard there is found;
He beats the world in catching "flies,"
   And covering the ground.
And as the Pitcher of our nine,
   Whene'er 'tis best to change,
The man will find that plays behind,
   That "Asa" has the range.

CHORUS.

And lest the boys should thirsty get
   When after balls they've ran,
We take with us, where'er we go,
   A jolly "Waterman."
Upon Third Base he stops hot balls,
   And sends them in so fine,
That all have said that jolly "Fred"
   Is home upon the nine.

CHORUS.

Our Shortstop is a man of worth,
  We hope he'll never die;
He stops all balls that come to him;
  He's grim death on the "fly."
The many deeds he has performed,
  We will not here relate,
But tell you now that "Johnny How"
  As a player is first-rate.

CHORUS.

The infield now is traveled o'er;
  The out comes next in line,
And "Moses Grant" is brought to view,
  Right Fielder in our nine.
He knows the place, he plays right well,
  To none the palm he'll yield;
He's bound you shan't catch "Moses Grant"
  A "napping" in right field.

CHORUS.

There is a man upon our nine,
  To him a verse we'll sing;
You all have heard of him before,
  His name is Rufus King.
Just now he plays as Center Field,
  Sometimes as Second Base;
We all have proof that merry "Ruf"
  Is worthy of the place.

CHORUS.

Come, fill your glasses to the brim
  With joyous, sparkling wine,
And drink a toast to all that's "Left"
  Of the 'riginal First Nine.
Of all the men who first essayed
  Upon that nine to play,
There's only one, and that's "Johnson,"
  Who holds a place to-day.

CHORUS.

To win the game we play to-day,
  We earnestly shall try,
And hope our expectations won't
  Be captured on the "fly."

We shall expect a quick return
To toss the ball around;
We'll welcome all to games of ball
Upon our "Union Ground."

CHORUS.

5. Pros—And Their Cons

Baseball's popularity was nationwide by 1869. There were over 1,000 organized clubs playing by then, and it was no secret that many of them employed professional players. In fact, it appeared that the only organization that could not see the developing phenomenon was the NABBP, even as dozens of its member clubs threw cash, no-show jobs, and other perks at their so-called amateur players.

The illusion of pure, innocent amateurism in the sport was important to the NABBP, which feared that cranks would become disillusioned and stay away in droves if they knew the extent to which money now was controlling the game. In actuality, any serious fan of baseball during this time period was well aware that most, if not all, of the game's top stars were receiving some sort of compensation from their clubs. And, any serious fan during this timeframe also was well aware of the extent to which gambling and hippodroming affected the outcome of hundreds of contests each season. The national pastime had a clear taint to it.

The NABBP finally ended its head-in-the-sand approach in the winter of 1868–69 when it repealed its law prohibiting professional players from playing in matches between association clubs. In its stead, the NABBP adopted a rule that divided its members into two separate classes—professional and amateur. NABBP Rule 5, Section 7 now read: "All players who play base ball for money, or who shall at any time receive compensation for their services as players, shall be considered professional players; and all others shall be regarded as amateur players."[1] Member clubs now could actively recruit professional players and, conversely, players-for-hire could solicit work from association clubs.[2]

A club was considered professional if a majority of its starting nine players were compensated. Amateur teams were allowed to employ a professional to manage or instruct them, but the professional could not play in any game without the consent of the opposing squad, and the opponent then would be allowed to field a professional of its own if it so desired.[3]

While the move was a logical one by the NABBP, it was lambasted by many in the media of the day. The *New York Times* called the move a "radical change," and added that "the evil influences which have apparently become a necessary connection of some professional clubs will render it questionable whether at all times this class of players will exert themselves to their utmost to win, and hence much of the interest which would otherwise attach to their contests will be wanting. This cannot occur either in the case of college nines or those of amateur clubs, for the 'esprit du corps,' and the natural rivalry between leading colleges to carry off the palm for their Alma Mater, must necessarily lead to legitimate efforts to win in every contest."[4]

The *New York Clipper*, however, took an opposing view, opining that professional baseball was a good idea because it would improve the quality of play, since professional players would have more time to practice and hone their skills, so as to be able to compete at the game's highest level of competition.[5]

The *New England Base Ballist* also favored the recognition of professionals, believing that this would thwart the use of paid ringers in strictly amateur contests. The *Base Ballist* further added that the less savory aspects of the game, such as gambling, hippodroming, no-show jobs, and revolving, would cease to exist if players were paid to play the game.[6]

Albert G. Spalding weighed in: "How could it be right to pay an actor, or a singer, or an instrumentalist for entertaining the public, and wrong to pay a ball player for doing exactly the same thing?"[7]

The majority of the sporting press, however, was opposed to the recognition of professionals. The *Paterson Press* of New Jersey bleakly predicted that soon, "every member of the first class nines of the country will be a paid professional player, and hundreds of our young men will aim at such a position as one of the most shining pinnacles that fame can boast."[8]

From a societal standpoint the elite and aristocratic class of American society also disliked the concept of professionalism invading the sport. They believed that baseball should be played only by gentlemen, and that it should be a leisurely pursuit, engaged in for purposes of exercise and pleasure only, and never for pay. If playing skill, and not pedigree, became of prime import, it was feared, then the sport would be overrun by the unwashed masses. It was enough to make one's blue blood run cold. One's lineage, race, color, and condition of servitude should be the determinant factors in whether one played baseball, according to the prevailing aristocratic thought of the day.

At the other end of the societal spectrum stood the gamblers, who controlled crooked baseball players like marionettes on a string. Ironically, both the societal elite and the gamblers shared the same opinion about professionalism in the game. Both opposed it, but for vastly different reasons. While blue bloods were class-oriented in their opposition to paid players, gamblers looked at the change from a strictly dollars-and-cents angle. If a player was being paid to play baseball, then he was less likely to be amenable to bribery, or so most gamblers believed. In essence, the gambling world of the day believed that a player would follow only the direction of whomever was paying him, be it a club owner or a gamester. It was an issue of control and influence, and the gaming world saw its grip on the sport weakening as players joined the professional ranks.

Albert Spalding, in commenting on the gambling element, observed:

> They had so long been a controlling influence, that anything threatening their ascendancy was sure to meet with stubborn resistance. Of course, their chief interest in Base Ball was that they could make out of it in the line of their nefarious profession. They feared that if the executive control of the game passed into the hands of men who also had cash at stake, it was a sure thing that just in so far as the management made money they must lose. They knew, of course, that the clubs must depend upon gate receipts for their income; that gate receipts depended upon the restoration of public confidence, and that public confidence could only be won by the eradication of the gambling evil.[9]

6. To Be Purely Professional

With the word that the NABBP had recognized professional clubs, Aaron Champion set out to create a championship-caliber team. It would not be an easy task, though, as all of the top clubs in the country now were breathlessly inking the game's top stars to contracts, and praying that the signees did not jump ship the moment that another club waved more dollars at them.

As the new year of 1869 dawned and people skated on the frozen-over Union Grounds, Aaron Champion recruited George Ellard and Alfred Gosham to assist him in signing up players for the 1869 Red Stockings lineup.

Ellard and Gosham zealously pursued their assignment, making it their goal to sign each and every player named to the 1868 *New York Clipper* Gold Medal team to a Red Stockings contract. The *Clipper* squad was the nineteenth-century equivalent of the All-Star team today. Imagine attempting such a feat in today's market! A modern-day club would bankrupt itself before it got out of the infield, let alone trying to sign an entire All-Star roster. Nonetheless, that was the goal of Ellard and Gosham at the outset.[1]

The duo found out quickly enough about the difficulties adherent to such a quest. Money, of course, was the main obstacle. The Red Stockings had ended the 1868 season $6,000 in debt and also had assumed all of the indebtedness of the Union Cricket Club related to the Union Grounds. Now they were issuing another stock offering in order to meet expenses and refurbish the Grounds. In addition to the financial crunch, Ellard and Gosham also quickly realized that they were not operating in a hardball vacuum, and that the other heavyweight clubs — the Athletics, the Mutuals, the Unions, the Atlantics, and others — were not about to stand pat and let this upstart Cincinnati squad monopolize all of the top talent in the game. A signing frenzy quickly developed, as clubs warred with each other in their quest to ink the greats of the nineteenth-century game to contracts.

For the players, it was a bonanza. They would hold themselves out to the highest bidder and frequently would revolve to another club if a better offer came along even after a contract had been signed. Aaron Champion, George Ellard, and Alfred Gosham all quickly learned that molding a championship-caliber Red Stocking club was a far more difficult task than they expected it to be, and they soon decided to let Harry Wright take charge of recruiting and signing ballplayers for the 1869 club.

Wright immediately went to work and began to religiously study newspaper accounts and team scorebooks as he tried to craft a top-shelf club for the '69 campaign. Many players wrote to Wright seeking a position with the Cincinnati nine, and Harry would dash off a response if he was interested in pursuing matters with the prospective Red Stocking. Wright once gave the following response to a prospective player who had written him for advice on how best to prepare for a career as a professional ballplayer: "In regard to diet, eat hearty Roast Beef rare with ... regularity, keep good hours, and abstain from intoxicating drinks and tobacco ... be a sure catch, a good thrower — strong and accurate — a reliable batter; and a good runner, all to be brought out ... by steady and persevering practice."[2]

The most startlingly dramatic aspect of Harry Wright's mission, however, lay in the decision that he, Aaron Champion, and the board of directors of the Cincinnati Base Ball Club made: to make each and every member of the 1869 Red Stockings a professional player. Up until that time, no club ever had been fully professional. Many teams, including the Red Stockings, had one or even a handful of paid players, but in the brief history of the game there had never been a club that consisted totally of professionals.

As the ice softened on the Union Grounds and the snow in the Queen City began to melt away, Harry Wright went about his business and slowly began to put together a club for the upcoming season. At the same time, he made a dramatic public announcement to the nation's sporting press: the Cincinnati Red Stockings of 1869 would be the first all-professional baseball club in the history of the game.

7. Throwing Down the Gauntlet of Defiance

Harry Wright and the Cincinnati Base Ball Club already were aware of the mainly negative response to the NABBP's decision to allow any professional players in association games, and the response to an all-professional club was similarly adverse. Many NABBP member clubs slammed the Red Stockings for the decision to be all-professional, claiming that it would make players into bloodless mercenaries and would destroy the game just as it was beginning to blossom into nationwide popularity.

Some of the negativism, however, clearly was attributable to jealousy by some of the more financially strapped clubs. The Red Stockings' chief rivals in the Queen City, the Buckeyes, blasted the Cincinnati Base Ball Club decision to be all-professional in an article in the *Philadelphia Sunday Mercury* shortly before the start of the 1869 season. Buckeye officials wailed that the pockets of other club members would be "taxed for those whose only interest in the club was their weekly salary," and further added that "you may rest assured that the Buckeyes will not be troubled with 'revolvers' who carry their pockets filled with offers from clubs, thereby keeping a club in a 'stew' from the beginning to the end of a season."[1] The article, however, conveniently failed to mention that the Buckeyes too had spent the winter of 1868–69 anguishing over whether or not to turn professional, lest they lost a competitive edge to the Red Stockings. Additionally, the Buckeyes were worried about a possible decline in attendance at their games as fans opted to watch the more talented professional nine compete across the city.

The harshest blow dealt the Buckeyes occurred shortly thereafter, when two of their star players — second baseman Charlie Sweasy and outfielder Andy Leonard — signed with the Red Stockings for the 1869 campaign. The Buckeyes, who did not have a wealth of cash to begin with, now did not even have any drawing cards to compete with the Red Stocking professionals. They had been done in by the dollar-waving Harry Wright, and it rankled the Buckeyes to no end. Given this turn of events, as Sweasy and Leonard left to don scarlet hose, the Buckeyes attempted to save face by righteously announcing that they would not defile themselves by accepting filthy lucre in return for playing baseball; rather, they would remain as pure, untainted amateurs.

Albert Spalding, however, saw fit to remark of the 1869 Red Stockings club that it "threw down the gauntlet of defiance to the National Association of Base Ball Players — not by a flaming pronunciamento, but by manly declaration that henceforth it would be known as a professional organization."[2]

In all, Harry Wright signed ten players to contracts for the 1869 campaign. The highest-paid player was George Wright — Harry's younger brother — who had been lured away from the Morrisania (NY) Unions, for whom he had been a *New York Clipper* Gold Medal recipient. Harry Wright signed brother George to a contract for $1,400 for the season. Harry himself was the second-highest-paid Red Stocking at $1,200 for the year. The Club's other starters earned between $800 and $1,100 for a season's work, while the lone salaried substitute, Dick Hurley, was inked to a $600 pact.

The Red Stocking players were making good money by 1869 economic standards. By way of comparison, the average skilled worker of that day earned approximately $525–$750 annually. The Red Stockings' contracts ran from March 15 to November 15.

The following men made up the 1869 Cincinnati Red Stockings roster.

Asa Brainard

Asa Brainard was the talented and temperamental pitcher for the '69 Red Stockings. He stood 5 feet 8 inches tall and weighed 160 pounds, with deep-set eyes and a mustache that connected to a set of thick muttonchops. Brainard already had established himself as a top-flight second baseman and pitcher with the Brooklyn Stars, Brooklyn Excelsiors, the Knickerbockers, and the Washington Nationals — where he formed a keystone combo with George Wright in 1867 — before Harry Wright convinced him to sign with the Red Stockings in 1868. Harry Ellard called Brainard "the most graceful and terrific pitcher that had ever gone to the box up to that time."[3] Many believe that the term "ace," as used in modern times to describe a topnotch pitcher, is a derivative of the name "Asa," and that when a club referred to its pitcher as its "ace," it meant that said pitcher was the team's best hurler, or its Asa Brainard.

Brainard's actual nickname was "The Count," and he was one of the first real characters in the game. Brainard was a night owl, and it was not uncommon to find him roaming the streets of a city in the wee hours of the morning, seeking any sort of excitement, often with a wide-eyed teammate in tow.

He carried his eccentricities with him to the pitcher's point, as well. Once, while Brainard was hurling, a wild rabbit suddenly darted across the diamond right in front of him. "The Count" eyed the wayward hare and, totally forgetting about the batter and the men on base, took the baseball and fired it at the little cottontailed beast. The rabbit darted out of harm's way as

After defeating the New York Mutuals by a score of 4 to 2 on June 15, 1869, the Red Stockings became nationally known. *Frank Leslie's Illustrated Newspaper* featured the carmine nine in a full-page layout in its edition of July 17, 1869. Center: Harry Wright. Clockwise from top center: Andy Leonard, Charlie Gould, Cal McVey, Doug Allison, Asa Brainard, Fred Waterman, Dick Hurley, Charlie Sweasy, George Wright (NATIONAL BASEBALL LIBRARY).

Brainard's errant toss bounded into the crowd, and all the while the two baserunners scampered around the bags and scored a pair of tallies. George Wright summed "The Count" up well when he said that Brainard "got odd notions."[4]

Asa Brainard, however, was a great pitcher. He would cross his legs, placing his left toe behind his right foot, take a single step forward, and then fire the ball homeward. He was a hard thrower, and he also was one of the first pitchers to effectively master the curveball.

"The Count" was not the most disciplined athlete in the world, and occasionally he would have Harry Wright pulling out his whiskers in frustration over Brainard's antics. Wright expected Brainard to pitch essentially every game, particularly since the hurler in that day stood only forty-five feet away from the striker and normally threw underhanded. Brainard, however, was something of a hypochondriac and, particularly after a long night of howling in the streets of a newly discovered city, would frequently show up at the ballpark with bloodshot eyes and a ragged look about him, complaining of a "sore arm" or some other imaginary ailment. On many occasions Harry Wright would pitch in Brainard's stead and beguile strikers with his famous "dewdrop" curve, but in more than one instance Harry ordered "The Count" to dress for the game and get out onto the field or face a docked paycheck. Harry's threat usually worked as the magic elixir that would quickly cure Brainard of any of his "ailments." "[Brainard] will shirk practice," Wright once wrote an associate, "but a little plain talk, 'play or no pay,' is usually effective."[5]

Brainard later would marry into the family that published the famous "McGuffey Readers" series. While playing for the Red Stockings, Brainard boarded with the family of William T. Truman, who had been one of the original partners in the printing firm of Truman & Smith, which published the First and Second Readers prepared by Dr. William H. McGuffey.

Upon William Truman's death, however, his family suffered financial reversals, and his widow, Elizabeth, found it necessary to take in boarders like the quirky Red Stocking twirler.

While lodging with the Truman family, Brainard developed smallpox. The Trumans' daughter Mary acted as Brainard's in-house nurse during his period of infirmity. "The Count" fell in love with Mary and they were married at the Truman home on Pike Street in Cincinnati.

Asa Brainard's 1869 salary was $1,100.

Doug Allison

Doug Allison was the gritty Red Stocking backstop from Manayunk, Pennsylvania. He was 5 feet 11 inches, 160 pounds, batted and threw right-handed, and worked in the off-season as a marble cutter and brickmaker.

Allison had played left field for the Masonic Club of Manayunk and had caught for the Philadelphia Gearys before signing with Cincinnati. Allison apparently was something of a rustic in his days prior to joining the Red Stockings. The first time he stayed in a hotel while playing for the Masonic Club of Manayunk, he sat in his room all morning, waiting for breakfast to be served to him there, even though he had never placed an order. He just assumed that someone from the hotel would deliver it to him in his room.

The Red Stockings literally stumbled upon Allison by accident. Cincinnati Base Ball Club officials John Joyce and Alfred Gosham were in Philadelphia in 1868 on a scouting mission when Joyce decided to catch a nearby ballgame. Doug Allison happened to be catching in the contest, and handled himself quite adeptly behind the plate. He also hit a long home run to straightaway center field in his initial at-bat in the game. Joyce quickly was sold on this backstop phenom. After the match, Joyce introduced himself to Allison and took him back to the Continental Hotel in Philadelphia where Joyce and Gosham were staying. As Allison waited in the hotel lobby, Joyce rushed upstairs and burst into the hotel room, telling Gosham, "Alfred, I've got him!" The two of them then went back downstairs, got Allison a haircut and a new suit, and brought him back to Cincinnati.

As was the case with all catchers of that era, Allison took an incredible beating each game. Allison stood directly over the plate for much of a game and used no glove, mask, chest protector, shin guards, or any other equipment as he handled Asa Brainard's spinning and velocitous offerings, although Albert Spalding wrote in 1911 that Allison had a Cincinnati saddle maker craft a small glove for him in 1869.[6] Allison likely shunned use of any such mitt in that first all-professional season, however, in order to avoid ridicule from other players. Accordingly, he frequently was maimed by foul tips, errant swings, thrown bats, and runaway baserunners barreling in on him. By season's end, Allison's collection of gnarled, mangled fingers and chipped teeth bespoke the hazardous position he played on the 1869 Red Stockings. The *Daily Alta California*, a San Francisco newspaper, called Allison "the best and most sure ball-catcher" in the land.[7]

Allison's 1869 salary was $800.

Charlie Gould

First baseman Charlie Gould was the only native Cincinnatian on the 1869 Red Stockings, and he also was the only six-footer on the historic nine. His lanky frame and his long arms allowed him to cover more ground around the bag than any other first baseman of his era.

Gould began his playing career in Cincinnati with the Buckeyes in 1863, and he stayed with them through 1867 when he crossed to the Red Stockings. While with the Buckeyes, Gould once won a baseball-throwing competition by launching a ball 302 feet 3 inches.

The affable, goatee-sporting Gould was nicknamed "The Bushel Basket" for his proficiency in the field. It was rare to see Charlie Gould muff a ball. Gould spent his off-seasons toiling as a bookkeeper in his father's butter and egg business on the banks of the Ohio River in the Queen City.[8]

Gould's salary for the year 1869 was $800.

Charlie Sweasy

Charlie Sweasy was the wiry second baseman with loving cup ears.

Sweasy hailed from Newark, New Jersey, and he began his baseball career with the nines of Newark and Irvington. Harry Wright pried "Sweaz" away from the crosstown rival Buckeyes in what proved to be a severe blow to the Red Stockings' arch-antagonists.

Sweasy was known to have a rather ornery disposition at times, an irascibility apparently brought on by frequent imbibition. He worked as a hatter during the wintertime when he wasn't guarding second base for Cincinnati.

Like Allison and Gould, Sweasy pulled down $800 for his 1869 play.

George Wright

Shortstop George Wright was the superstar of the 1869 Cincinnati Red Stockings, and arguably was the best ballplayer of that era. The *New York Clipper* gushed that George had "the reputation of covering more ground than any other player in the country. He is very active, a swift and accurate thrower, and especially excels in 'judgment,' as it is called, never being bewildered at the most critical moments in a contest."[9]

George was born on January 28, 1847, in Harlem, twelve years the junior of his brother Harry. Like his sibling, George started out as a cricketer at the St. George Cricket Club. He easily made the transition from cricket to baseball and in 1863, while only sixteen years old, latched on with the New York Gothams club and competed against ballplayers twice his age. In an interview given early in the twentieth century, George Wright recalled the following about his early days:

> I used to see the St. George team play cricket at the Red House in the early '50s, and in 1857 the club went to the Elysian Fields in Hoboken, where I saw my first baseball game. The teams playing there comprised the Knickerbockers, Gothams, Eagles, Empires, Mutuals, Actives, and several other New York

clubs. They were composed of New York businessmen who went to Hoboken two or three times a week for exercise and recreation, and quite frequently, having heard that I was interested in the game, invitations were extended to me to play.

I played in every position, and [later] I became a regular member of the Gothams. First I was their catcher, but one day a foul tip struck me in the throat and it hurt me so much that I never afterward was able to muster up sufficient courage to catch, and so I went to left field, eventually going to second base and then to shortstop.

We used to wear long trousers tied at the bottom with skate straps, blouses, caps, and canvas shoes with iron spikes.[10]

George was a powerful batsman, an agile fielder, and a speedy runner. He frequently would stage juggling exhibitions with a ball and bat prior to a game, much to the delight of the grandstand crowd. George was the first roving shortstop in the game; he would roam between second base and third base instead of remaining stationary behind the pitcher, as was the norm of the day. He also played a deep shortstop, positioning himself at the back of the baseline, instead of closer in on the skin of the infield. George's fandom would joyously exclaim, "I'd rather be Wright than President!" every time their hardball hero snared a hot daisy-cutter with his bare hands.

"He fielded hard chances barehanded and fielded them with either hand and could throw with either arm," George's later teammate, James "Deacon" White, would say of him. "My, how he could throw without hesitating — scoop up the ball and throw with the same motion and run to any part of the field for hard chances, too."[11]

In 1867 George Wright was the prize infielder for the Washington Nationals. The Nats toured the nation that summer and lost only one game all season, to the Forest City nine of Rockford, Illinois, which featured star hurler Albert Spalding. One of the highlights of Wright's 1867 campaign was his club's 53-10 drubbing of brother Harry's Red Stockings. While the shellacking humiliated Harry, it also made him realize his younger brother's greatness as a player. George jumped to the Morrisania Unions of New York in 1868, but Harry made him the prize signing for the '69 Red Stockings.

"In 1869 the Reds engaged me to go to Cincinnati," George Wright later told an interviewer. "They were eager for a championship team in Cincinnati in those days, and it was this club that first made contracts with its players, and its players were also the first to wear short trousers. I had made up my mind that to be a successful baseball player a man should stick to one position, and so I played at short all the time I was with the Reds, except to pitch a few innings."[12]

George Wright was a pleasant and jovial fellow, with an angular face, curly hair, and large teeth. George kept his pearly whites intact by occasionally sporting a primitive mouthpiece while playing in the field—one of the first, modest examples of protective equipment in the game. Albert Spalding lauded George's "sunny disposition, athletic figure, curly hair and pearly white teeth, with a good-natured smile always playing around them, no matter how exciting the game."[13] The *St. Louis Republican* called George "the beau-ideal of base-ball players. His fielding exhibits science at every point, his picking, throwing and strategy could not be excelled, and he is plucky in facing balls of every description.... He is personally very quiet, modest, and possessed of that trait unusual with base-ball players—thrift."[14]

The *New York Clipper* paid homage to Wright's legendary fielding prowess with the following account:

> It is recorded that some years ago two men were on the bases when the batsman struck a high ball over George Wright's head. He ran back, and succeeded in getting beneath it, although in an awkward position. The ball was seen to strike his hands and bound out again. The two men on the bases were intently watching him, and the instant they observed this slip they started on a dead run each for the base ahead of him, the batsman being already so close to first base that it was impossible to cut him off. The bound of the ball from George's hands, however, was a little trick of his, and before it could reach the ground he caught it a second time. This, of course, was a genuine catch, and put out the batsman, while the two men on bases had no right to run until the ball had settled in his hands. With no suspicion, however, of the artifice both were far off their bases, and before they could return the ball was thrown to second, thence to first, and thus the whole three men were put out, a triple play of an extraordinary character.[15]

In recalling the spectacular Wright in 1904, *The Sporting Life* observed, "Whenever he would pull off one of those grand, unexpected plays that were so dazzlingly surprising as to dumbfound his opponents, his prominent teeth would gleam and glisten in an array of white molars that would put our own Teddy Roosevelt and his famed dentistry far in the shadow."[16]

George Wright earned a salary of $1,400 in 1869, making him the highest-paid player in the club.

Fred Waterman

Fred Waterman was a slightly built (5 feet 7½ inches, 148 pounds), balding, part-time insurance salesman with a thick, droopy mustache. He was from New York City, and he patrolled the hot corner for the '69 Red Stockings. Waterman's hardball career had begun in 1864 with the New York Empires. In 1868, he was one of the recipients of a Gold Medal from the *New York Clipper*.

Waterman was nicknamed "Innocent Fred" due to his guileless appearance, but this belied the fact that he also previously had played for Boss Tweed's notorious New York Mutuals club, where he was supposed to be examining cadavers in the city coroner's office when he really was snaring grounders for the Tweed nine at the Brooklyn, New York Union Grounds.

Waterman's 1869 salary was $1,000.

Andy Leonard

Andrew Jackson Leonard was born in County Cavan, Ireland, but was raised in Newark, New Jersey. Leonard and fellow Garden Stater Charlie Sweasy took similar routes on their way to the Red Stockings: both toiled for the highly regarded Irvington Club of New Jersey in 1867, then both bolted to the Cincinnati Buckeyes in 1868, and Harry Wright plucked both of them from his Queen City rivals for the 1869 hardball campaign.

The *St. Louis Republican* called Leonard "one of the 'Class A' of outfielders. In all respects he is superior, being a perfect judge, a sure catch, and a wonderful long thrower."[17] The *New York Clipper* added that "as regards accuracy of throwing, Leonard at left field has no superior. He has so repeatedly thrown in the ball from that position to the home plate with such unerring precision that the runner on third base has not dared attempt to reach home."[18]

While unarguably a top-shelf flychaser, Leonard also could be temperamental in his relationships with his teammates and his manager. Harry Wright, in an 1875 letter, detailed how Leonard and Cal McVey, the Red Stockings' right fielder, "dislike exceedingly, when playing in the field, to be told to change their positions when certain players come to the bat.... [They] seemed to think it was a reflection on them or on their judgment as players, when told by the pitcher or captain to change or move in the field."[19]

Andy Leonard's 1869 salary was $800.

Harry Wright

Center fielder Harry Wright wore several hats for the 1869 Red Stockings. A team's manager in that era played a different role than he does in today's game. In 1869, a manager was responsible for all of the off-field responsibilities that today would be performed by a general manager, traveling secretary, and public relations department. Harry Wright, in his role as manager of the Red Stockings, was responsible for scheduling all games (Wright would send out hundreds of letters and telegrams to fellow managers to arrange game dates and gate share agreements), making all of the club's travel arrangements, negotiating hotel rates on the road, purchasing equipment, arranging for groundskeeping duty at the ballpark, distributing checks to all of the Cincinnati players, talking to the sporting press that followed the club, and promoting the Red Stockings so that cranks in Cincinnati and everywhere else would come out and buy a ticket to watch his all-professional nine.

In his role as captain of the Red Stockings, however, Harry Wright engaged in the strategic aspects of the game which is the hallmark of the baseball manager of the modern era. Harry positioned players, made pitching and fielding changes, gave hitting and baserunning signals, and led his charges in pregame drills and batting practice. Whenever one of his players performed especially well in a ballgame, Harry would present the Cincy standout with a "property bouquet"—an idea that Wright had borrowed from the theater of his day.[20] The Cincinnati newspapers faithfully reported every presentation of a property bouquet to a player, which brought added publicity to Harry's red-legged nine.

Essentially, Harry Wright not only chased flies in center field, but also acted as a one-man front office for the '69 Red Stockings. In addition to all of his other duties, he also meted out discipline and fines when necessary, and also negotiated all player contracts.

The *New York Clipper* lauded Harry as "admittedly the best captain that ever took a base-ball or organization in hand. He is a thorough disciplinarian, and can reflect that he has always been the leader of a corps of gentlemen against whom no word of suspicion has ever been uttered."[21]

In a later interview with the *Sporting Life*, Harry Wright discussed his managerial philosophy:

> I try to impress upon my players the fact that the people who come to see them play, whether it be at home or abroad, want to see base ball. If they cannot win, let them never cease trying until the last man is out, no matter how large the task may be. A careless play is never excusable. The men should work just as hard when they are ten, fifteen, or twenty runs behind as when the score is a tie. Then if the game is ultimately lost no fault can be found with them on the score of indifference. If the players always work on this principle they will overcome many obstacles which for the time being might appear insurmountable.[22]

For his many duties, Harry Wright earned a salary of $1,200 in 1869.

Cal McVey

Cal McVey was a stocky piano maker from Montrose, Lee County, Iowa, who patrolled right field for Cincinnati. The *New York Clipper* called him "a long thrower and terrific batsman."[23] He and Charlie Gould were the only two Midwesterners on the club.

Prior to joining the Red Stockings, McVey toiled for the University, Western, and Active baseball clubs in the Indianapolis area. It was during an 1868 game between the Red Stockings and the Actives that Harry Wright first noticed McVey and his hardball talents, and Wright immediately set out to sign him up with Cincinnati for the coming season.

Cal McVey was the baby of the '69 Red Stockings; he was only eighteen years old when he started the season for them and, in fact, Harry Wright had to get permission from McVey's father before the talented teenager was allowed to move to Cincinnati to join the Red Stockings.

McVey also was something of a daredevil gymnast. According to the *Boston Times*, the Red Stockings' flychaser was "a born acrobat and acquired considerable proficiency in his early days turning Catherine wheels and handsprings over the rapids of the Mississippi. [McVey would] turn a flip-flap every time his club won."[24]

While McVey was the youngest and most acrobatic of Harry Wright's troupe, he also was the strongest, earning money on the side as a prizefighter of some renown. Not surprisingly, he also was one of the first Red Stockings to leap into the fray anytime a fracas broke out during a game. Of course, sometimes it appeared as though McVey would be squaring off against one of his own teammates rather than an opposing player. Harry Wright recalled how both Leonard and McVey disliked being told to change position in the field and, according to Captain Harry, McVey occasionally would

> get ugly and show his temper.... He says that he has played in the field long enough and knows the strikers well enough to know when to change his position without being told. [In a game played at Worcester, the pitcher] motioned to McVey to move around for some certain player that was at the bat. [McVey] got very indignant and told [the pitcher] to go to hell, that he knew how to play his position and that he had ... all he could do to attend to his pitching. This I learned afterwards and gave McVey a good talking to about it.... [McVey} remarked, 'It is some of your cricket notions, you never see it done by any other club.' [I took it as] quite a compliment ... although he didn't mean it as such.[25]

For his 1869 play, McVey earned $800.

Dick Hurley

Substitute outfielder Dick Hurley was signed by Harry Wright as the lone backup to the Red Stocking nine. Hurley, who had attended Columbia

University, also was the only left-handed batter on the club. Hurley had spent the 1868 season with the Cincinnati Buckeyes but, like Andy Leonard and Charlie Sweasy, switched Queen City alliances when Harry Wright came calling with pen and contract in hand.

That contract included an 1869 salary of $600.

Other Players

Only the sunniest optimist believed that ten players would be sufficient for an eight-month-long season. Over the course of the '69 campaign, as injuries dictated, Harry Wright would sign other area ballplayers to contracts on a one-game or as-needed basis. Dave Birdsall, a rail-thin, 126-pound outfielder who had played with George Wright in 1868 at Morrisania, was among those recruited by Harry Wright to fill in on a day's notice. Oak Taylor and a third baseman named James Bradford were other Cincinnati replacements, as was a catcher named Fowler, who occasionally replaced Doug Allison behind the plate as the battered Red Stocking backstop tended to broken fingers, smashed toes, chipped teeth, and other hazards inherent to his miserable position on the field.

All ten players signed by Harry Wright to Red Stocking contracts were veterans — players who already had established themselves as stars in the NABBP. This was done intentionally. George Wright, in an 1883 interview with the *Boston Daily Globe*, waxed poetic on the reasons behind such a philosophy: "The raw material exerts a depressing and demoralizing influence upon the veteran players, and this tends toward defeat. There should be a studied unity of action observed among the members of a club while a game is in progress; each player should be acquainted with the methods and style of the others. These elements, which are so necessary to success, are of course lacking when you bunch a lot of raw material with that which has been thoroughly seasoned, and a warping of the whole must follow."[26]

1869 Base Ball — The Rules of the Game

The rules of the game in 1869 were far different from the current set. While the nine position players were the same, the pitcher stood only forty-five feet from home plate and generally threw the ball underhanded. The catcher could stand anywhere behind the plate he so desired. Some backstops, like Doug Allison, stood directly behind the plate and took a nasty beating over the course of the season. Other catchers of the era would stand as far as fifty feet behind the batter, which was much safer, but a lot less meaningful in terms of defensive positioning. Most catchers did, however, move almost directly over the plate when there was a runner on base.

The second baseman generally played directly behind the second-base bag, leaving a huge gap between first base and second. Most shortstops played close behind the pitcher, although George Wright was an exception, positioning himself at the back of the baseline.

The first and third basemen generally played very close by their respective bags because of the "fair-foul" rule in existence at the time. Any ball hit fair that then rolled foul before reaching the first-or third-base bag was still considered a fair ball, and in play. Today, such a ball would be foul. Due to this rule, the first and third sackers straddled the bag so as to be ready to pounce on any dribblers that started out fair and then darted foul. It was not uncommon for some first and third basemen even to position themselves entirely in foul territory while in the field.

The home plate umpire stood behind and to the right of the plate. The game's official scorer also was positioned on the field, between home plate and the first-base bench area.

The ball itself was not as lively as that used in today's game, but it was just as hard. The sphere was furnished by the challenging club, and became the property of the winning nine. No gloves or any other type of hand protection were worn by any player. Broken and mangled fingers were commonplace in the gritty game of 1869. As mentioned, catchers who stood directly behind the plate took the worst beatings, and teams replaced their backstops more than they did at any other position, including pitcher.

There was no pitcher's mound in 1869. Rather, the era's hurlers worked from a six-foot-square area called the "pitcher's box"—as in the current phrase, "He was knocked out of the box"—in the midst of which was the "pitcher's point," a flat, circular iron plate, white in color, from which the pitcher delivered his offerings. The pitcher in 1869, as mentioned, stood only forty-five feet from home plate. The pitcher essentially threw underhanded in that era. According to NABBP rules; "The ball must be pitched, not jerked or thrown, to the bat. The ball shall be considered jerked if the pitcher's arm touches his person when the arm is swung forward to deliver the ball; and it is a throw if the arm is bent at the elbow at an angle from the body or horizontally from the shoulder when the arm is swung forward in delivery. A pitched ball is one delivered with arm straight and swinging perpendicularly [Note: The NABBP probably meant to say "parallel," instead of "perpendicularly," here] and free from the body."[27]

The home team did not always bat last as is the custom today; it varied from game to game, and would be decided by a coin flip. There was no wide, skin infield as exists today. Rather, the skin part of the infield was narrower and more rectangular in shape. Fielders generally caught the ball with their hands held in a "clamshell"-style position, with both sets of digits cupped out-ward in the direction of the oncoming ball. Bats generally were much larger than they are today. The first bats were cricket bats, but by the 1860s many players wielded a cumbersome, 3½-foot war club that resembled a wagon tongue and was fashioned out of willow, elm, or ash.

The game in 1869 was much more geared toward the batter — then known as the "striker"— than the pitcher. The striker could take a base on only three called balls. The striker could tell the pitcher exactly where to place the ball, such as low and inside, or across the letters, or however the striker liked it. If the pitcher did not place the ball where the striker directed, the umpire could call out a warning, "ball to the bat," and then the umpire could call balls on each ensuing wayward delivery. Strikes were never called on the first pitch thrown to a striker unless he specifically swung and missed. An umpire never issued a called strike until after the striker was warned of the penalty for refusing to swing at appropriately placed pitches. Only after giving such a warning could the umpire call strikes on well-placed pitches at which the striker did not offer.[28]

The ballparks of 1869 — commonly referred to as grounds — usually were fenced in, although the phrase "fenced in" in those early days of stadia did not have the same connotation as it does today. In many instances, "fenced-in grounds," according to the nineteenth-century understanding of the phrase, merely meant that a split-rail fence had been erected some distance behind the outfielders and around the perimeter of the entire grounds as a means of keeping the often-boisterous cranks of the day from crashing the gate and/or storming the field while a game was occurring.

The umpire's lot in the nineteenth-century game was a treacherous one. He worked the game frequently in a top hat and morning coat, and gener-ally was not paid for his duties. The umpire of that era was heavily abused and assaulted, both verbally and physically. Pictures from this time period show arbiters being pelted with rotten fruit and vegetables and being attacked by rowdy cranks on a regular basis. One cartoon from this era showed an umpire perched in a cage above the field, safely out of harm's way as a mob of enraged players and cranks shook their fists and hollered at him from below.

The game and its players were rougher and feistier than today's brand. Players from the Red Stockings' era reveled in the way they fielded without gloves or other protection, and in their later years would deride the modern players who were so cowardly as to have to wear a glove on their hand for protection and fielding ease. George Wright, commenting on the state of the game of baseball in 1915, observed: "[The] game today [in 1915] is much faster than it was.... This is due mainly to the use of gloves. All the time I played Baseball I never wore a glove. Now I will tell you something that will probably cause Tris Speaker and the other outfielders to raise a howl of protest. I don't believe outfielders should be allowed to wear gloves today."

"Modern" ballplayers, even in 1915, could never measure up to the old-timers.

8. A Blazing Scarlet in the Spring

The media of the day basically treated the all-professional 1869 Cincinnati Red Stockings as a novelty and an interesting story, but few if any preseason prognosticators actually gave them a chance of being a top-notch competitor, despite all of their winter additions. The New York Mutuals and the Philadelphia Athletics were favored by most of the sporting press to tangle for the game's brass ring, although the *New York Clipper* did observe that "contestants for the championship ... will have to keep one eye turned towards Porkopolis."[1]

The '69 Red Stockings engaged in one final pursuit prior to the start of the season so as to make themselves stand out among NABBP clubs: they were outfitted with stylish new uniforms.

Prior to the garb sported by the '69 Red Stockings, the typical baseball uniform consisted of a woolen cap, a flannel shirt, and long trousers. Fashion guru Harry Wright decided, however, that his club needed new duds, and he hired Mrs. Bertha Betram, a Cincinnati seamstress who perhaps should be recognized as the Betsy Ross of baseball, to put together the Red Stockings' new uniforms.[2]

The uniform shirt was soft collared and flared at the neck, with a bib centered on the front which was stitched a red, Old English-style "C." The shirts were half-sleeved and were laced at the throat by drawstrings. The jerseys were white in color, and were made of a material called, ironically enough, cricket flannel.

Harry Wright decided to make a bold fashion statement with his choice of pants. He vetoed the idea of long trousers, and instead opted for white, cricket flannel knickers featuring a below-the-knee clasp. The Red Stockings were the first club in baseball history to wear knickers. Each player also sported a leather belt and belt buckle that was adorned with the same Old English "C" featured on the uniform tops.

The real attention grabbers, however, were the long, bright red stockings sported by the players. Harry Wright opted for the brilliant scarlet hosiery as a dashing symbol of his ball club and its nickname. Margaret Truman, sister of Asa Brainard's bride Mary, knitted the historic hose. The two Truman sisters also stitched baseballs for the club, since machine-stitched spheres were scarce and expensive.

The Red Stockings' caps were white and jockey-style in appearance. The players wore Oxford shoes made of calfskin, with sharpened brass spikes attached to the bottom of them. The footwear extended up over the ankle, which, one supposes, made the Red Stockings the first club to sport high-tops.

Henry Chadwick described the Red Stockings' garb as a "comfortably cool, tasteful" uniform.[3] In order to save on expenses, Harry Wright ordered uniforms in only three standard sizes. No customizing was done; this way, worn-out attire could be replaced quickly and inexpensively, so as to keep equipment costs down. The Red Stockings had started a definite hardball trend by basing their team name on a stocking color; soon thereafter, they were joined in the NABBP by other similarly designated squads, including the Chicago White Stockings, the New York Mutuals (nicknamed the Green Stockings), and the Washington Olympics (nicknamed the Blue Stockings).[4]

As springtime blossomed on the banks of the Ohio River, the winter snow melted away and the renovations on the Union Grounds were completed. The Union Grounds ballpark contained wooden grandstands that extended from behind home plate and down the first- and third-base lines. A wooden club-house situated behind the third-base grandstand was reserved for exclusive use by club members and their guests. The Red Stocking players normally arrived at the ballpark already in uniform and thus did not use this clubhouse in order to change into their game flannels. Adjacent to the clubhouse was a ladies' pavilion known as the Grand Duchess. Next to the Grand Duchess's cupola was a large platform where Zouave bands frequently performed, much to the enjoyment of the crowds inside the Union Grounds.

A small steeple adorned the grandstand roof, and a Red Stocking pennant, mounted to a flagpole, whipped in the breeze. There were no dugouts at the Union Grounds; players sat on wooden benches right in front of the crank-filled grandstands, which left the baseballers vulnerable to jeers, catcalls, and an occasional overripe tomato.

Inside the Union Grounds, hungry hardball cranks could choose from such ballpark delicacies as popcorn, peanuts, ice cream, Cracker Jacks, chocolate, chewing gum, sandwiches, beer, and even whiskey, all served by concessionaires from local restaurants who carried their comestibles in large baskets with leather straps.

On April 17, 1869, the Cincinnati Red Stockings took to the Union Grounds for their first game as the first all-professional club in baseball history. The Red Stockings were pitted against a "Picked Nine" club, that being a squad of local standout players, akin to an amateur all-star team.

Harry Wright penciled in the following batting order for the Red Stockings: 1. George Wright, shortstop; 2. Doug Allison, catcher; 3. Charlie Gould, first base; 4. Fred Waterman, third base; 5. Harry Wright, pitcher; 6. Andy

Leonard, left field; 7. Asa Brainard, right field; 8. Charlie Sweasy, second base; 9. Dick Hurley, center field.

The Red Stocking strikers erupted early, plating five runs in their first at-bat of the new season. The first six strikers reached base in the inaugural inning, including four via Picked Nine errors. The Red Stockings scored runs in every single inning of the game, and came away with a 24–15 victory over the Picked Nine. The two Charlies — Gould and Sweasy — were the hitting stars, as each cracked four safeties. Andy Leonard and George Wright both walloped sixth-inning homers. The Picked Nine, which was tapped as the Red Stockings' inaugural opponent, could not have been selected for reasons of fielding prowess: the squad dropped six fly balls and muffed another six grounders. The squad's catcher, Spencer, meanwhile, was charged with a half-dozen passed balls.

Despite the victory, the local press was less than enthusiastic in its review of the Red Stockings' opening triumph. The *Cincinnati Enquirer* yawned, "The baseball season for 1869 was opened yesterday by a game between the first nine of the Cincinnati Club and the field. The playing on both sides was very poor. There was quite a large number of spectators present, but the enthusiasm of last summer was lacking."[5]

A week later on April 24 the Red Stockings met a similarly styled Picked Nine, and once again the Stockings romped, 50–7. Harry Wright juggled his lineup somewhat, tabbing Asa Brainard to pitch and also moving Dick Hurley to first base, Cal McVey to right field, and Captain Wright himself out into the center-field pasture.

The highlight of this contest was the Red Stocking sixth inning, when they sent twenty-seven strikers to bat and scored twenty-three runs. The Wright brothers each cracked three hits in the sixth inning alone. George Wright finished the day with nine hits and seven runs scored. Asa Brainard had a no-hitter going into the eighth inning before Picked Nine shortstop Lowe singled to break it up. Once again, this Picked Nine squad was an absolute sieve in the field, as catcher Lowe was charged with ten passed balls, pitcher Beckler tossed three wild pitches, and third baseman Barnes — a one-man disaster area — muffed one ball, made another bad throw, and also was charged with three "slow handlings" that allowed Cincinnati strikers to reach base. For good measure, the Picked Nine's outfield troika missed four fly balls.

The *Cincinnati Enquirer* reported the day after:

> The return game between the Red Stockings and the chosen nine was played yesterday afternoon at the Union Grounds, the weather being very fine and the grounds in excellent condition. The game was a brilliant one, though the result shows quite a disparagement in the skill of the combatants. The attendance was quite large — a decided improvement upon the number present at the opening game, but we noticed a lack of that intense excitement so frequent

at those long to be remembered and hotly contested games of last summer, and we ascribe as the cause that as yet only local players have taken part, and our citizens have not that home pride as they, in seeing their old favorites carry off the laurels.[6]

On May 4, the Red Stockings met the Great Western Club in their first official game of the year. The city of Cincinnati was in a festive mood that day as Harry Wright's boys rode out to the Union Grounds in a caravan of fancy, ribbon-adorned carriages, behind which followed hundreds of merry cranks, eager to see whether their boys could measure up to the first real competition of the season. The Red Stocking players strode confidently into the Union Grounds and onto the emerald-hued field, resplendent in their crisp, white flannel uniforms and blazing scarlet hosiery, and marching nine abreast across the field, like soldiers in formation on their way into battle.

The Red Stockings did not disappoint their loyal legions that afternoon, trouncing the Great Westerns 45–9. George Wright led off the Cincinnati first inning by cracking his second home run of the season, and seven of the first eight Red Stocking strikers reached base as the carmine club notched seven tallies in the game's first frame. Harry Wright was back pitching, and he moved Asa Brainard out into center field for the contest. Once again the Cincinnati opposition was totally inept in the field: the not-so-Great Western nine committed twenty-seven errors, including seven dropped flies and a dozen other assorted muffed balls.

Six days later the Red Stockings tangled with the Kekionga nine of Fort Wayne, Indiana, at the Union Grounds. The *Cincinnati Enquirer* called the Kekiongas "a very fine looking set of young men.... When they appeared on the ground, dressed in the neat uniform of blue pants, white shirt and blue cap trimmed in white, they were loudly cheered."[7]

The Red Stockings, however, continued to wreak hardball havoc as they obliterated their stylish opposition 86–8. In the second inning of the mismatch, Cincinnati scored fourteen runs as Doug Allison, Andy Leonard, Asa Brainard, Charlie Sweasy, and George Wright each clocked a prodigious roundtripper. After five innings, the score already stood at 61–4. The Red Stockings scored runs in every inning, and plated at least ten runs in four of the game's nine frames. George Wright probably could have played against the Kekiongas all by himself, and still would have won: the star shortstop wound up with eleven hits on the day—three home runs, five doubles, and three singles—and twelve runs scored. Cal McVey—the ninth batter in Harry Wright's lineup—cracked ten hits and scored nine times. Asa Brainard got the victory, helping himself out at bat by launching a pair of circuit clouts. The Kekionga contingent committed a mind-boggling twenty-four errors in the debacle, including a dozen by its disastrous double-play duo of Dawson and Bacon.

"During the greater part of the game," the *Cincinnati Enquirer* noted, "[the Kekionga players] appeared to be somewhat non-plussed, and as a consequence many fine plays which they are undoubtedly capable of making were allowed to go by default."[8] It's hard to think of a more diplomatic way to say that the Kekionga boys booted two dozen balls over the course of nine very long innings.

The Red Stockings next bashed the Antioch College nine 41–7, and it appeared that each Cincinnati opponent was attempting to outdo the prior one in terms of setting some sort of mark for fielding incompetence. The Antioch crew managed to commit an astonishing thirty-two errors that afternoon, including nine by the second baseman, Bellows, and eight by the third baseman, Elliott. The Red Stockings, by way of comparison, committed four miscues in the contest.

"From the score we append it will be seen that the Cincinnatis had an easy victory," the *Cincinnati Enquirer* concluded in a fit of understatement.[9]

On May 22, the Kekiongas, apparently undeterred by the 86–8 obliteration suffered at the hands of the Red Stockings twelve days earlier, met the sons of Harry Wright in a rematch. Considering the catastrophic result of May 10, it had to be a moral victory for the Kekionga nine on this occasion, as they fell by a score of only 41–7.

There was a blight on the Red Stockings' easy victory over the Kekiongas, however, as Doug Allison was forced to leave the game with an ankle injury. Dick Hurley went into the game as Allison's replacement, but Harry Wright wished a speedy recovery for his starting backstop, knowing that he would need Allison behind the plate when the Red Stockings met the iron of the NABBP.

The Great Western Base Ball Club also returned to the Union Grounds in late May, seeking revenge for the 45–9 thrashing they suffered in the Red Stockings' first real game. The Cincinnati BBC heavily promoted the contest in the Queen City's newspapers, hoping for a big gate to offset some of the smaller crowds that had turned out for the scarlet nine's early matches.

The game was scheduled for Decoration Day — which since has become Memorial Day — and so all the city's stores and businesses were closed, which gave Aaron Champion and company even more reason to hope for a large turnout. Decoration Day, however, also was opening day for the horse racing season at nearby Buckeye Park, and so once again only a few hundred hardball partisans were scattered throughout the grandstand at the Union Grounds.

The Red Stockings sprinted out to a lightning-quick 35–5 lead after only two and a half innings on the grey and dreary Decoration Day afternoon, when suddenly the skies above opened up and an intense downpour soaked the Union Grounds. The field quickly became saturated, meaning the cancellation of the contest and — much to the chagrin of Aaron Champion — forcing the Red Stockings to refund money to all of the ticket holders inside the Grounds. Because only two and a half innings had been played between the Red Stockings and the Great Westerns — far short of the five-inning minimum required for an official game — the Cincinnati BBC lost out on approximately $60 in gate receipts on the soggy Decoration Day afternoon.

9. Looking to the East

After spending the first six weeks of the 1869 season essentially at home, the Red Stockings packed their bags at the end of May to begin a four-week eastern road trip, where they would face the iron of the NABBP. The Red Stockings were not in the pink of financial health as they got ready for the tour. Reports surfaced that the club already was $6,000 in debt at this point in the season, even after two more special stock subscription campaigns. Aaron Champion allegedly had to appeal to some of his wealthy friends and club members in the city for additional backing for the team. One club member, Will Noble, reportedly loaned the Red Stockings his wife's $300 life savings to help the ball club out of its financial crunch.[1]

Harry M. Millar, who was a local baseball reporter for the *Cincinnati Commercial*, accompanied the club on the journey. Aaron Champion actually had lobbied for Millar to follow the club eastward and was delighted with the arrangement, particularly for publicity reasons. Millar, in addition to filing newspaper reports about each game, also acted as a part-time scorekeeper for the club. Finally, and of most importance to Champion, he flashed the results of each contest over telegraph wires back to the Commercial Hotel in Cincinnati, where hundreds of hardball-hungry cranks would gather to await word of how the Red Stockings had fared. Essentially, Harry Millar was more of a publicity flack for the club than he was a hard-nosed reporter.

On May 30, Aaron Champion, John Joyce, Harry Millar, Harry Wright, and the Red Stocking players gathered at the Gibson House in downtown Cincinnati. Harry Wright prohibited any player from leaving the hotel once he arrived, desiring that the nine be well rested for the trip. Asa Brainard, of course, showed up at the hotel already soused.

Inside the hotel, Aaron Champion exhorted his troops to carry on in their winning ways, and added that the better they played, the larger the crowds would likely be that turned out to see them, and the higher the gate receipts would be in which the club would share. That proved to be enough of a financial incentive to send all but the most sociable of the Red Stockings scurrying for their beds.[2]

At 7:00 A.M. on May 31, the Red Stockings' traveling party boarded a train at the Little Miami Railroad station in the eastern section of Cincinnati. The club packed two dozen bats and a dozen balls for the tour, plus one bottle of arnica, a concoction used to treat bruises, cuts, and sprains.

That same day, as the Red Stocking express roared out of the Little Miami Station, Cincinnatians picked up their copies of that day's *Cincinnati Commercial* and read a glowing article by Harry Millar that, while meant more as hype than as keen analysis, nonetheless would prove to be amazingly accurate.

"The nine," Millar gushed, "has had plenty of exercise and practice, and is so well regulated that it should avail itself of its capabilities of defeating every club with which it contests."[3]

10. The Journey Begins

The first stop on the Cincinnati tour was Mansfield, Ohio, for a tilt with the Independent Club. When Harry Wright arrived at the Fair Grounds on that afternoon of June 1, he looked up into the wooden grandstands and grimaced. There were few spectators to be found. This meant, of course, that there would be a paltry gate share for Cincinnati at the conclusion of the game.

Enraged at the lousy Mansfield turnout, Harry Wright and his red-legged crew took out their aggression on the Independents, throttling the home club by a score of 48–14, with Harry himself the winning pitcher. Every time one of the Red Stockings connected with the ball, the sound echoed throughout the nearly empty ball yard, which only served to further infuriate Wright. Afterward, the Independent manager handed Harry a check in the amount of $50, which represented Cincinnati's anemic gate share for the afternoon.[1] It was hardly enough to cover the hotel bill. From a financial standpoint, it was a disastrous start to the Red Stockings' East Coast swing.

Things did not improve the next afternoon in Cleveland, where the Cincinnatians bombed the Forest City nine, 25–6. Once again, the crowd was less than what Aaron Champion or Harry Wright would have hoped for. The only bright spot on the afternoon was a mammoth home run by George Wright, which he blasted clear out of the fenced-in Forest City Ground. Doug Allison also was back behind the plate, having recovered from the ankle injury he suffered on May 22 in the 41–7 victory over the Kekiongas, and was able to razz his brother Art, the Forest City first baseman, about the shellacking handed the Clevelanders by the Queen City nine.

The Red Stockings' share of the game's gate receipts was $81, more than what they received for the Mansfield game, but still far short of what Aaron Champion and Harry Wright were hoping for.[2] The first two games of the eastern tour had been on-field successes, but financial disasters.

As the Red Stockings' steam locomotive chugged eastward late that evening, Harry Wright rubbed his forehead, then his eyes, and stared out at the moonlit countryside and breathed a loud sigh. The club had a payroll to meet and expenses to pay, and there was no way that the tour could be sustained for very long if no one showed up to watch the Red Stockings play ball.

The weary band of baseballers finally pulled into Buffalo at 4:00 A.M. the next morning, worn out from the long train ride through the night. For most of the players, their only desire was to go directly to the hotel to get some rest before that afternoon's tilt with the Niagara BBC. Asa Brainard, however, had other plans. As the rest of the Red Stockings sleepily boarded the carriages that would take them to the hotel, Brainard grabbed Fred Waterman — "Innocent Fred" — and convinced him to tag along on an early morning romp through the streets of Buffalo.[3] Harry Wright was none too pleased about Brainard's early morning adventure — with less than twelve hours to go before game time — and he excoriated Brainard for it, and also for being such a bad influence on Waterman. Undeterred, The Count and Innocent Fred bounded off into Buffalo's downtown section, full of thirst and curiosity, as the purplish sky overhead cracked golden with the first rays of morning.

The Red Stockings arrived for that afternoon's match with the Niagara nine in a horse-drawn coach complete with upholstered benches for the spike-shod travelers. Harry Wright was encouraged to finally see a packed house on the tour, as Buffalo cranks packed the house at Niagaras Field.

The Niagaras took a 2–1 lead after the first inning, which was the first time all season that the Red Stockings had trailed in a game at any point. The Queen City pros stormed back with five tallies in the second, though, and a dozen more in the fourth, and cruised to a 42–6 triumph over the battered Buffalonians. The *Cincinnati Enquirer* modestly called the contest "one-sided."

Leaden skies greeted the sons of Cincinnati the following afternoon in Rochester as they arrived at the local grounds for a match with the Alert Base Ball Club. Rain had become as much a nemesis to Aaron Champion and Harry Wright as any opposing nine could be, for if a game was canceled due to inclement weather, then all of the ticket money would have to be refunded to the cranks, and the Red Stockings would have to walk away from the park empty-handed — an occurrence with which the club was becoming all to familiar.

More than 3,000 Rochester partisans jammed the grounds — which doubled as a public square — and watched the Red Stockings plate two runs in the first inning. The Alerts, however, responded with a pair of their own to tie the contest. Suddenly, just as the Red Stockings prepared to bat in the second inning, the skies above opened up and a short but intense deluge soaked the field and sent all of the players and fans scurrying for cover. Because there was no grandstand on the grounds under which to seek shelter, many of the Red Stockings and Alerts ran across the square to a nearby house, banged on the door there, and begged to be let in to escape from the showery elements.

Harry Wright stood inside the house, safe from the storm, but miserable. It was as if there was a curse on the tour, he must have thought. If this game was called off, it would be the fourth in five games for which the Red Stockings would have little to show in the team's purse.

The downpour finally ended, but the Alert field was saturated. Even the Alert groundskeepers were not budging to try to dry the field off. Harry Wright was disgusted. He could not afford to lose any more gate receipts on the trip. Suddenly, he whirled around to his teammates and ordered them to grab every available broom they could find. Harry even grabbed one himself, and a startled Alert fandom looked out onto the field to see the mighty Cincinnati Red Stockings themselves sweeping all of the water off the soaked diamond. Harry then grabbed a couple of buckets of sawdust and spread the absorbent over the muddiest areas of the field.[4] His groundskeeper chores completed, Harry marched over to the Alert bench and informed the home club that their grounds now were usable. The Alerts reluctantly agreed, and play was resumed. Rejuvenated, the Red Stockings returned to bat and notched five runs in the second as they want on to a soggy 18–9 conquest in rainy Rochester.

The next day in Syracuse, circumstances working against the Red Stocking tour reached the zenith of absurdity. The Stockings landed at the Salt City ball grounds to joust with the Central City BBC, but the Cincinnati lumbermen must have thought that they mistakenly had been given directions to the local dump instead. Harry Wright absolutely could not believe what he saw. The Syracuse grounds were nothing more than an overgrown patch of unkempt brush, with weeds and wild grass sweeping high against the players' scarlet hose. The outfield fence was partially dismantled.

Suddenly, a shot rang out, startling the Cincy baseballers and sending many of them running for cover. Harry Wright spun around and looked out into the outfield, where some riflemen were peering and pointing up into the overcast mid-afternoon sky. From the heavens, a small, plump, grayish object plummeted toward the earth, and landed with a small and feathery thud elsewhere on the scrubby grounds. One of the sharpshooters hustled over to where the fallen prey had landed, scooped it up, and stuffed it into a bag he carried. Harry walked over to him, introduced himself and his club to the hunter, and inquired as to the whereabouts of the absent Central City nine.

"What is happening here?" the Red Stockings' manager asked the hunter. "Where is the Central City club?"

The hunter just looked at Harry and shrugged his shoulders. "I don't know," he responded. "No one said nothing to me about any ballgame. The grounds are being used all afternoon for a pigeon shoot."

Harry was stunned. A pigeon shoot! He disgustedly looked around at the ballfield with its foot-high weeds and grass, and not a single Syracuse hardballer to be found anywhere. Harry had made arrangements back in early April with the Central City club for this match, but word obviously had never reached him regarding its cancellation. All Harry knew was that here he was, in the middle of a hardball wilderness in Syracuse, surrounded by a flock of dead pigeons, and with nothing but empty stands and another empty purse to show for it. When it rains, it pours, Harry Wright must have thought — and one surely had hit the skids when it was pouring pigeons! In consolation, Harry and the rest of the Red Stockings ventured to a nearby health spa by Onondaga Lake that featured salt spas at thirty-five cents apiece.[5] There, the sons of Cincinnati soaked their sorrows in salinity over another lost payday.

The Red Stockings continued their New York swing by riding the New York Central rail line to Troy, where they outslugged the Haymakers and their star pitcher, Cherokee Fisher, 38–31, in a match witnessed by some 10,000 Troy cranks. This was the type of crowd that Aaron Champion and Harry Wright had longed to see on the tour. The Red Stockings grabbed $281 in gate receipts on the afternoon, and the red ink flowed a little more lightly in the club's ledger books.

The only drawback to the victory was a sprained ankle suffered by Andy Leonard in the fourth inning of the win. The gutsy left fielder refused to be removed from the game, however, and stayed in for the entire nine innings, hobbling out four hits and five runs scored in the contest.

The next day in Albany, though, Leonard's ankle swelled, and the plucky flychaser was howling in pain. While Leonard remained on the bench and applied arnica to his injured wheel, super-sub Dick Hurley replaced him in left for the matchup against the National Club in the Empire State's capital city. Charlie Gould clouted a two-run homer in the first inning to give the Red Stockings an early lead, but the Nationals stormed back with eight unanswered tallies over the next three innings to grab an 8–7 lead. In the fourth inning, though, the Cincinnatian's first ten batters all reached base and they scored a dozen runs to retake a 19–8 lead. The Red Stockings added another dozen tallies in the sixth inning and fifteen more in the seventh. At the end of the seventh frame, with Harry Wright and company ahead 49–8, the game was called so that the Cincinnati crew could rush to the Albany train station for that evening's journey to Springfield, Massachusetts. George Wright notched seven hits in the Albany slugfest, including three doubles and two triples. He also scored seven runs. Fred Waterman likewise collected seven safeties and scored seven tallies. Dick Hurley proved his worth as a valuable fill-in, as he struck a half-dozen hits, including two roundtrippers. Between the fourth and seventh innings of the Albany contest, Hurley stroked five connective safeties.

The Cincinnati hardballers next stormed into Springfield on the afternoon of June 9 and annihilated the Mutual Base Ball Club by a score of 80–5, before only 200 stalwarts at the city's Hampton Park.

It was probably just as well that so few cranks witnessed this massacre.

The rout commenced immediately, as the first six Red Stocking strikers reached base in the first inning and the club posted eleven runs. The Red menace continued their attack with eleven more tallies in the fifth, and they also stole seven bases in that frame. The trouncing continued in the seventh as Cincinnati plated another sixteen men, and Harry Wright personally heisted four bases himself over the course of two at-bats in the inning.

The Carmine rampage continued in the eighth with another eleven runs. In the game's penultimate frame, the Cincinnati nine swiped an incredible fourteen bases off the beleaguered Mutual backstop. Charlie Sweasy swiped four bags of his own that inning, including home plate. One batter after Sweasy's home heist, Cal McVey also filched home plate. In the ninth inning, Doug Allison — the lead-footed catcher — also stole home to highlight another thirteen-run Red Stocking outburst.

Almost every Red Stocking striker that afternoon had better personal statistics than the entire Mutual ball club. George Wright laced eight hits in thirteen at-bats, scored eleven runs, and swiped eight bases. Fred Waterman went eight-for-twelve with nine runs scored and a half-dozen heists. Harry Wright likewise was eight-for-twelve with nine runs scored, but the Red Stocking manager/captain pilfered eight bags, including his quartet in the seventh inning. Charlie Gould notched a half-dozen safeties and eight base poaches. Even Cal McVey, the ninth-place striker in the potent Cincinnati lineup, cracked a half-dozen hits and had five stolen bases, including his eighth-inning home plate theft. Harry Wright and his teammates swiped an inconceivable forty-nine bases that afternoon against the hapless Mutuals, as the scarlet-hosed speedsters wore holes in the soles of their Oxford high-tops.

The *Springfield Daily Union*, in a fit of understatement, remarked: "That was not what would be called a brilliant game of base ball on the Park ... simply for the reason that the Red Stockings had it all their own way and went through the Mutuals like 'suds through a sink'."[6]

The sons of the Queen City next trekked to Boston for a tilt with the Lowell Base Ball Club on Boston Common on June 10. One Boston paper reported that "the Cincinnati men are all large in frame, with fine muscular development."[7] Playing on the same field used by British soldiers as a training ground during the Revolutionary War, the Stockings romped 29–9. To the Lowell BBC and its Boston fans, the invading army on this occasion wore red hose instead of red coats.

Two days after their Boston Common joust, the Red Stockings crossed over the Charles River into Cambridge to battle the Harvard College Base Ball Club at the College Ground, in a matchup of Red versus Crimson. The Queen City pros took the collegiate lads to school that afternoon with a 30–11 lesson in Professional Hardball 101.

The Red Stockings also were scheduled to tangle with the Yale College nine two days after the Harvard contest, but a day-long shower in New Haven forced cancellation of the matchup, and even the industrious Harry Wright and his crew of cricket-flanneled groundskeepers with their brooms and sawdust could not thwart the precipitative Mother Nature that day.

The rainy skies, of course, soaked the Red Stockings' wallets as much as they did the rest of the city of New Haven that day. Because of the cancellation of the game and the loss of another day's gate receipts, Aaron Champion and Harry Wright were forced to borrow $245 from Harry Millar of the *Cincinnati Commercial* in order to meet club expenses.

A steam locomotive pulled out of the black and drizzly New Haven railroad station that evening with an anxious troupe of Red Stocking ballplayers on board. For Harry Wright and his band of unblemished Cincinnati baseballers, the time had come to invade New York City.

11. The Gotham Showdown

The Big Apple was home base for three of the top clubs in the game; the New York Mutuals, the Brooklyn Eckfords, and the Brooklyn Atlantics. If Cincinnati was to be recognized as one of the elite nines in the sport, it would have to prove it against this potent troika. For Harry Wright and his mates, the road to success ran straight through Gotham.

The first test for the Red Stockings came on Tuesday, June 15, as they prepared for battle with the New York Mutuals at Brooklyn's Union Grounds. The rain from the previous night had ended, but slate-hued, tenebrous storm clouds still hung low over the borough, and an unseasonably brisk wind whipped off the East River and across the Union Grounds field.

The streets surrounding the ballyard were clogged with Mutual cranks who had arrived by ferry, carriage, and even skiff. The congestion was exacerbated when several arklike, wooden brewery wagons, loaded with dozens more New York cranks and drawn by teams of six horses, rumbled up to the Union Grounds gates to drop off their bands of beery Mutual partisans.

Over 10,000 Mutual rooters packed into the Union Grounds. Among the New York partisans sat club owner William March, "Boss" Tweed, the notorious Gotham politico who had stashed his ballplayers onto the city payroll in a variety of no-show jobs. Back in Cincinnati, some 2,000 Red Stocking partisans jammed into newspaper and telegraph offices and the lobby of the Gibson House Hotel to await Harry Millar's telegraph reports on the big game.

The Red Stockings took the Fulton Street Ferry across the gray and choppy East River to Brooklyn and disembarked in Williamsburg. From there the Cincinnati squad climbed into a large wooden coach that the Mutuals had provided for their transport to the Union Grounds.[1]

Asa Brainard, whose delivery the *New York Daily Tribune* called "beautiful, easy, and true,"[2] got the starting nod from Harry Wright, and as he and his red-legged teammates warmed up before the game, New York cranks taunted them with the cry, "Wait 'til you play the Mutuals — they'll show you a thing or two!"

Harry Wright had a particularly personal desire to whip the Mutuals, for their top player was John Hatfield, who previously had toiled for Wright and the Red Stockings but had jumped from the club after a contract dispute. Wright wanted to show Hatfield his error in revolving away from Cincinnati. The Mutuals, conversely, were overjoyed to be able to pencil Hatfield into their lineup, and confidently predicted victory over the upstart Cincinnati nine because the Mutuals believed that Hatfield would be able to intercept all of Harry Wright's hand signals to his mates.

A coin flip was held to determine who batted first. Harry Wright called it correctly, and allowed the hometown Mutuals to bat first in this tilt. The New Yorkers were shut down by Asa Brainard in their initial at-bat. In the bottom of the first, Fred Waterman reached base on an error by John Hatfield — much to the delight of chortling Harry Wright — and then took second base on a passed ball, and then scored when Mutual shortstop Dave Eggler let a Doug Allison grounder bounce off of his leg and into the outfield. Cincinnati took a quick 1–0 lead.

The Red Stockings increased the lead to 2–0 in the third when local hero George Wright led off with a double to left field and then scooted home when shortstop Eggler booted another grounder, this time off the bat of Fred Waterman.

Asa Brainard, meanwhile, was handcuffing the Mutual strikers, and the tempestuous twirler carried a precarious 2–0 lead into the top of the eighth inning when New York's ninth-place batter, right fielder McMahon, led off with a two-bagger and scored on a John Hatfield safety to cut the Cincinnati lead to 2–1.

A misty twilight settled in over the city as the Mutuals batted in the top of the ninth inning, their last chance to avoid defeat at the hands of the Red Stockings. Dick Hunt led off for the Tweed men and lined an Asa Brainard offering over Charlie Sweasy's head into right-center field for a safety as the previously dormant New York cranks suddenly stirred to life.

The next striker, Marty Swandell, laced another single, also over the leap of Sweasy. The Mutuals now had two runners on, nobody out, and Charlie Mills approaching the plate. The lanky Mills called out where he wanted the pitch to be, and Brainard wheeled and fired. Another base hit! Hunt scurried home, Swandell cruised into second, and the game was now knotted 2–2, still with nobody out.

A weary Asa Brainard sighed heavily and rubbed the scuffed baseball in his meaty hands. The momentum was now entirely with the Mutuals, and they stood on the verge of taking the lead. Shortstop Dave Eggler strode cockily to the bat as thousands of boisterous New Yorkers in the stands hooted at Brainard. Eggler called out the placement of the ball and menacingly twirled his bat in anticipation. Brainard wiped his forehead and peered in at the Mutual slugger. He ground the turf-worn sphere into his hip, crossed his legs, took one step forward, and fired it in. Eggler swung mightily for the fences, but only sent a weak pop-up toward Fred Waterman at third base.

As the ball rose lazily into the darkening environs, Harry Wright shouted instructions to his infielders from his post in center field. "Two, Fred, two!" Wright hollered at his third baseman. Waterman intentionally let the ball fall in front of him, then pounced on it and fired it to George Wright, who had hustled over to cover third base. Wright, in turn, heaved it to Charlie Sweasy at second, and the Red Stockings had executed a head-spinning double play. The flawless twin-killing quieted the Gotham rowdies at the Union Grounds and gave Brainard a bit of breathing room. He still was sagging, though, and gave up a two-out base on balls to Mutual hurler Rynie Wolters, which put the lead run at second base. Right fielder McMahon strode to the plate, eager to be the toast of the city that evening. He waved his bat around at Brainard but could only manage a weak pop-up behind the plate, which was snared by Doug Allison after a long run, much to the relief of the bone-weary Brainard and his anxious mates.

The Red Stockings had barely survived the harrowing top of the ninth, but now they were in a position to win the game in their last at-bat. Andy Leonard led off and sent a ground ball skidding into left field, where flychaser Hunt muffed the spinning grounder and let it get by him. By the time he retrieved the ball, Leonard had turned the first-base bag. Hunt saw this, turned, and fired the ball over to Everett Mills. Leonard froze, too far off of the base. As Harry Wright groaned on the bench, Leonard raced back and forth between first base and second in a run-down before he was tagged out.

Pitcher Brainard next strode to the plate, barely able to keep the bat off his shoulder. He lined a Rynie Wolters offering down the third base line, which Marty Swandell snatched. As Brainard plodded toward first base, he watched as Swandell's throw sailed over Everett Mills' head. Rejuvenated, Brainard wheeled all the way to third base as the Mutuals chased down Swandell's errant throw. The Red Stockings now had grabbed the momentum back from the Mutuals and were in a position to win the contest. Charlie Sweasy approached the plate in the gloomy dusk and stared out at the suddenly frazzled Wolters. Brainard wiped his grimy hands on his flannel pants and took a short lead off third. Wolters heaved one in to Sweasy. Charlie Mills, the Mutuals' catcher, was preoccupied with watching Brainard dance off of third, and he let the ball graze off his hand as it sailed across the plate. A passed ball! Brainard lumbered home with the winning tally. Under 1869 rules, however, a team stayed at bat for the entire inning, even if the winning run already had scored. Sweasy, with the pressure off his shoulders, laced a triple and then scored on a wild pitch by the disconsolate Wolters, and the Red Stockings were triumphant, 4–2.

The victory rocked the Queen City. Thousands of joyous cranks spilled out of newspaper and telegraph offices and the Gibson House Hotel, and danced and drank in the downtown Cincinnati streets, giddy over the upset victory by their beloved nine. This was the type of win that Aaron Champion had craved — a tenacious, hard-fought triumph over a squad picked by many as the best in the game. The *Spirit of the Times* called the contest "the best-played game ever witnessed."[3]

That evening, back at Earle's Hotel in Manhattan, Aaron Champion and Harry Wright and all of the Red Stocking players relaxed in the lobby and received congratulations from cranks and reporters alike. "What a contest!" marveled Henry Chadwick, the most famous baseball writer of the era. "The Red Stockings are popularizing the game in the east like no other club has before!"

As Aaron Champion savored the afternoon's conquest over the Mutuals, he was handed a telegram:

> CINCINNATI, JUNE 15, 1869
> CINCINNATI BASE BALL CLUB, EARLE'S HOTEL, NEW YORK:
>   ON BEHALF OF THE CITIZENS OF CINCINNATI, WE SEND YOU GREETING. THE STREETS ARE FULL OF PEOPLE, WHO GIVE CHEER AFTER CHEER FOR THEIR PET CLUB. GO ON WITH THE NOBLE WORK. OUR EXPECTATIONS HAVE BEEN MET.
> ALL THE CITIZENS OF CINCINNATI,
> PER S.S. DAVIS[4]

Champion read the telegram aloud to the throngs gathered inside Earle's Hotel, and whoops and cheers rang across the crowded lobby. The Red Stocking players led more hurrahs and drank toasts until Harry Wright decided that the celebration was on the verge of leaving his club a little too soused for its next game, and he ordered his players to bed.

The New York newspapers were not as adoring toward Harry Wright and his upstart nine. Many Gotham scribes blasted the professionalism and the commercialism of the Red Stockings. The *Day Book* fumed that the Queen City pros were "at the beck and call of the sporting men, who bring them into the ring, gamecock fashion, and pit them against each other for money."[5] The *Day Book* conveniently omitted any mention of the dozens of Mutual ballplayers who larded the city's payroll at an annual cost of several thousand dollars to its citizens.

The following afternoon the sun reemerged and the Red Stockings ventured back across the East River to the Capitoline Grounds in Brooklyn for a match with the Atlantic Base Ball Club. Once again, over 10,000 New Yorkers squeezed into the new amphitheater. The game sold out, so thousands of additional cranks parked their wagons and carriages on the grass banks adjoining the field and prepared to watch the eagerly awaited contest from that vantage point. Hundreds more watched from trees and housetops near the grounds. One brave soul was even spotted straddling a church steeple, holding a lightning rod with one hand and peering into a set of field glasses with the other.

The Cincinnatians bounded out to a 5–0 lead in the first inning, and then they totally blew the game open with a thirteen-run outburst in the second frame. It reached 21–0 before the Atlantics even got on the scoreboard, and the Stockings cruised to a 32–10 rout. The *New York Daily Tribune*, impressed with the easy manner in which Harry Wright's club manhandled the Atlantics, noted that the Brooklyn nine seemingly were "an impenetrable wall [but the Red Stockings] easily … battered the wall down." The *Tribune* further observed how, after the contest was over, the previously cocky Atlantic cranks "quietly dispersed, pondering over the uncertainties of base ball."[6]

In the finale of their three-game Gotham swing, the sons of Cincinnati returned to the Union Grounds to joust with the Brooklyn Eckfords in front of another 8,000 New York cranks. Six straight hits in the third inning by Leonard, Brainard, Sweasy, McVey, George Wright, and Gould paced a seven-run frame, and once again the Red Stockings won a laugher, 24–5, to make it a clean three-game sweep in the Big Apple.

The *Daily Tribune* could only conclude about the Queen City invaders that "their strength lies in their unity — each fully understands each other's peculiarities of play, and acts accordingly."[7] It was enough to make Aaron Champion break into a huge smile as his club crossed the Hudson River and trekked into New Jersey for the next tilt. The Red Stockings had beaten the iron of the Empire State, and now had to be recognized as among the top clubs in the NABBP.

There also was another reason for Champion's felicity. After the financially disastrous start to the tour, the Red Stockings had reaped a profit of $4,474 over the course of the seven games in the state of New York, which was quite a respectable profit by 1869 standards.[8]

The mighty Red Stockings, gushed the *Spirit of the Times* in a report about their East Coast tour, "are the only true exponents of the game today. Full of courage, free from intemperance, they have conducted themselves in every city they visited in a manner to challenge admiration, and their exhibitions of skill in the art of handling both ball and bat call for unexampled praise. Their present tour has done more to elevate the game than any trip of the kind ever before known."[9]

12. "Oh, How Is This for High?"

In Irvington, New Jersey, on a hot sunny June afternoon, the Red Stockings tangled with that town's nine. Charlie Sweasy and Andy Leonard were both alumni of the Irvington club, and both were warmly received by the hometown crowd as they greeted old friends and signed autographs. The Cincinnatians coasted to another easy victory, 20–4, and staged another one of their clever double play schemes to boot. With Irvington runners on first and second and one out in the second inning, striker Stockman whiffed on a third strike. Doug Allison, however, intentionally muffed the ball, forcing Stockman to run to first. As Stockman bolted down the line, Allison fired the wayward sphere out to George Wright covering second base, and he in turn tossed it to Gould at first, for another innovative twin-killing. The bedazzled Garden State crowd sat stunned for a moment, and then broke out into appreciative applause for the Red Stockings' impressive on-field exploits.

It now was on to Philadelphia for Harry Wright & Co. for three games against heavyweight City of Brotherly Love squads. The Red Stockings torched the Olympic club 22–11 in their first tilt in the city, scoring runs in all but one inning of the game. On that same day, June 19, the *Spirit of the Times* published a glowing piece on the Queen City pros. The journal was impressed by the quiet leadership exhibited by Harry Wright, and observed how Wright was the only player on the field who spoke. The *Spirit of the Times* concluded that "steady, temperate habits and constant training are all conditions precedent to a first-class organization."[1]

The Red Stockings next faced the Philadelphia Athletics who, along with the New York Mutuals, were considered to be the cream of the hardball crop in 1869. Some 25,000 Philadelphians jammed into the Athletic Grounds for the contest and, as in New York, thousands more milled around outside. Resourceful carriage and coach drivers sold space on the top of their vehicles as "box seats" to those who could not get into the Athletic Grounds, and such crank-heavy wagons clogged the streets around the Philadelphia ballyard all afternoon.

The beginning of the contest was delayed by about thirty minutes as the two clubs debated which type of ball to use in the game. Harry Wright wanted to use the "Ellard" ball, made by Cincinnati sporting goods dealer George Ellard.

The "Ellard" ball was considered a pretty lively sphere for that era. The Athletics countered with the "Ross" ball, which had a little less juice to it. The Athletics argued that they had consented to using the "Ellard" ball in Cincinnati in 1868, and now should be allowed to use the "Ross" ball in turn. Harry Wright finally consented to the request, and the game began.[2]

Cincinnati again cruised to an early 17–3 lead, sparked by a nine-run sixth inning. In three at-bats over a two-inning span, George Wright cracked a pair of triples and a home run, for ten total bases in the three plate appearances, and the Stockings coasted to a 27–18 triumph. One game report noted that the Red Stockings, and particularly Doug Allison, fielded balls like Chinese magicians.

The Red Stockings now had conquered the top two clubs in the game in the New York Mutuals and the Philadelphia Athletics, and the cranks back in Cincinnati were ecstatic over the success of their nine and the glory that it brought to the fair Queen City. After the Athletics game, Aaron Champion received more telegrams:

> CINCINNATI, JUNE 21, 1869
> CHAMPION AND JOYCE, C.B.B.C., BINGHAM HOUSE, PHILADELPHIA
>   FINEST IN THE WORLD. PREDICTIONS TRUE. IMAGINE TWO THOUSAND PEOPLE IN AND AROUND THE GIBSON HOUSE WAITING FOR THE SCORE. EVERY MINUTE ROARS AND YELLS GO UP.
> OH, HOW IS THIS FOR HIGH/
> AL. G. CORRE
> (PROPRIETOR OF GIBSON HOUSE)[3]

> CINCINNATI, JUNE 21, 1869
> A.B. CHAMPION, PRESIDENT OF CINCINNATI BASE BALL CLUB
>   ALL HAIL THE VICTORS! THE UNION CLUB CONGRATULATES THE BOYS UPON THEIR BRILLIANT VICTORIES AND UNPRECEDENTED SUCCESS. GREAT EXCITEMENT THROUGHOUT THE CITY, AND THE NEWS OF YOUR VICTORY TO-DAY RECEIVED WITH GREAT JOY. PLAY CAREFULLY-HEAVY BETS PENDING UPON THE CLUB RETURNING HOME THE WINNERS OF EVERY GAME. A RED-HOT RECEPTION IN STORE FOR YOU. ALL THE WOMEN ARE WEARING RED STOCKINGS IN HONOR OF THE NOBLE NINE, AND YOUR PRAISE IS ON EVERY TONGUE.
> UNION CLUB[4]

The Red Stockings concluded their Philadelphia stay with a 45–30 slugfest victory over the Keystone BBC at the Athletic Grounds, which was located at the corner of Seventeenth and Columbia Streets in the city. The start of the game was delayed by an hour to let the field dry off from a morning shower. Cincinnati scored in every inning, and the Keystones were only shut out in one frame. It already was close to 7:30 P.M. when the seventh inning ended, with the Stockings ahead 45–30, and the game was called due to darkness. In

Harry Wright's mind, that was about the only correct call made by the umpire all day. The home plate umpire for the tilt was Philadelphia Athletics left fielder Ed Cuthbert, and it became apparent early on in the contest that anything close was going to be decided in favor of the Keystones. Cuthbert even went so far as to stop passed balls with his feet in order to assist the Keystone club in the game.[5] Despite having the arbitral deck stacked against them in this regard, the sons of Cincinnati still were able to prevail.

The Red Stocking caravan journeyed southward to Baltimore the next day for a tilt with the Maryland BBC at the Pastimes Grounds. A crowd of close to 5,000 cranks showed up for the game, a record in Baltimore at the time. The hospitable Maryland crew hung a large banner over the entrance to the Pastimes Grounds that read, "WELCOME RED STOCKINGS."

Harry Wright and Co., however, did not return the pleasantries. It was 29–0 in favor of Cincinnati before the outclassed Maryland crew even notched a single tally, and the Red menace romped on to a final score of 47–7. Charlie Gould rapped out seven hits on the afternoon and scored eight times. Both Wright brothers lined a half-dozen safeties. Asa Brainard, who got the victory, helped his own cause with three hits of his own.

June 25, 1869, was a Red-letter day for Harry Wright and his band of carmine-hosed hardballers. They arrived in Washington early that morning and were greeted at the train station by a welcoming delegation sent on behalf of the Washington Nationals nine. At the station, the Red Stockings piled into a magnificent coach pulled by four horses, and rode to the Willard Hotel in the city where hundreds of cheering Washington cranks greeted them upon their arrival there.

That steamy afternoon, the Stockings stomped all over the Nationals, 24–8, in front of a crowd of about 8,000 cranks that included dozens of government officials perched in the choice seats at the grounds. A couple of blocks away, on the roof of the State Department building, one crank watched the game through a pair of field glasses as he held an umbrella in his free hand to protect against the sun.

In the contest, George Wright led the Red onslaught with five hits, including two home runs, a triple, and a pair of doubles. He missed hitting for the cycle due to his own strength. Cal McVey also shone. The ninth-place batter in the potent Cincinnati lineup reached base in all six of his at-bats, and scored each time. After the contest, the Red Stockings gathered for a team portrait at the studio of noted Civil War photographer Mathew Brady.

The following morning presented one of the most memorable moments of the entire season for the Red Stockings. President Ulysses S. Grant had invited the entire club to the President's Mansion (the edifice would not be called the White House until 1902) for an audience on that steamy summer morning.[6]

The band of excited baseballers marched down Pennsylvania Avenue and into the President's Mansion for their meeting with Grant. The legendary Civil War general-turned-Chief Executive entered the room puffing on a large black cigar, and he was introduced to each member of the Red Stocking contingent individually. The president complimented each player on his sterling play that season, and noted how the *Washington Republican* had called the club's eastern tour the greatest in the short history of the game. "I believe you warmed the Washington boys somewhat yesterday," Grant cracked to the Red Stockings, causing all the players to break out in laughter.[7] Grant, who was having problems dealing with corruption in his administration, was the first president to attempt to improve his lowly standing among the citizenry by greeting a popular sporting team of the day.

Afterward, the giddy Cincinnatians bounded back out onto Pennsylvania Avenue and marched out to the National Grounds for that day's game. On the way, the happy hardballers broke out into song:

> We are a band of base ball players
>   From Cincinnati City,
> We come to toss the ball around
>   And sing to you our ditty;
> And if you listen to the song
>   We are about to sing,
> We'll tell you all about base ball
>   And make the welkin ring.
> The ladies want to know
>   who are those gallant men in
> Stockings red, they'd like to know.[8]

That afternoon, Cincinnati met the Olympic Club at the National Grounds in front of what one Washington writer called "the most aristocratic assemblage ... that ever put in an appearance at a base ball match."[9] The Stockings stormed out to a 4–0 lead after two innings, but the Olympic nine responded with three tallies of their own in the top of the fifth to keep things close. As the Red Stockings prepared to bat in the bottom of the fifth, a summer deluge soaked the nation's capital. The rain fell so hard and for so long that not even an attempt by Harry Wright and his broom-wielding and sawdust-tossing mates could salvage the grounds for any further play. Instead, the two clubs met in a rematch two days later, and the Red Stockings ran away — literally — with a 16–5 victory over the Olympics. Two of the first three Red tallies came on steals of home executed by Charlie Gould and Andy Leonard in the first and second innings of the tilt.

The final stop on the Red Stockings' East Coast tour was Wheeling, West Virginia, where the Cincinnatians were shellacking the Baltic Base Ball Club 53–0 before the contest was cut short by rain. The Stockings plated eleven runners in the first, including another heist of home by Charlie Sweasy, and added fifteen more tallies in the second. In the third it was worse yet for the beleaguered Baltics as Cincinnati launched an eighteen-run assault, highlighted by Charlie Sweasy's second swipe of home plate in three innings. In the fourth, probably suffering from exhaustion from wheeling around the Wheeling bases so much, the Red Stockings could only muster a paltry nine-run attack. Charlie Sweasy, though, stunned the Baltic nine by stealing home for the third time in the contest — and it was only the fourth inning! With the score already standing at 53–0, and the game not even half over, the rains that had followed the Red Stockings eastward began anew, and the home plate umpire stepped in and halted the proceedings.

The Red Stockings' offensive statistics in even such a rain-shortened contest read like something out of a Ripley's *Believe It or Not* tale. George Wright had eight hits (four singles, two doubles, two triples) in eight at-bats, scored eight runs, and stole six bases — all in a four-inning contest. Fred Waterman and Charlie Gould each cracked a half-dozen safeties in the four frames in Wheeling. The pilferous Charlie Sweasy, poacher of home plate on three occasions, wound up with a total of six stolen bags in his four innings of thievery.

It was a weary but content band of baseballers who headed back to Cincinnati that evening. Harry Wright and his boys had stormed the East Coast with a vengeance, winning all twenty-one games in which they had played. As the Red Stockings journeyed home, Harry Wright stared out at the black and drizzly countryside and smiled, remembering how gloomy things had appeared in the early days of the tour. That was all in the past, though; tens of thousands of cranks had since turned out to watch the mighty Red Stocking nine, particularly in the three big cities of New York, Philadelphia, and Washington. The club, in fact, had netted $1,700 on the eastern tour, making the swing a success both on the field and in the ledger books.[10] Now it was time for the unblemished sons of Cincinnati to return home to the fair Queen City.

13. The Glory of the Queen City

Upon the Red Stockings' arrival at the Little Miami Railroad Depot in Cincinnati, Harry Wright and his mates were mobbed by a boisterous throng of close to 5,000 adoring cranks. The crowd at the depot waved banners, tossed money, shot off firecrackers and guns, and broke out into a lively chorus of the club fight song. Some of the more flirtatious young women in attendance lifted their skirts several inches off the ground to reveal red hosiery, a surefire sign of a new type of attraction that Harry Wright's boys were receiving now that they were home again as conquering heroes.

The surprised but appreciative Red Stocking players were escorted to a caravan of carriages decorated with flowers, plumes, and ribbons that would make up part of a parade that would carry the players through the celebratory city.

As the noisy procession made its way out of the Little Miami station, Currie's Zouave Band broke out into "Hail to the Chief" in honor of the hardball heroes. Behind the band were two carriages filled with executives of the Cincinnati BBC and other local pooh-bahs, and then came the Red Stocking players themselves in their gaily bedecked carriages. Hundreds of merry cranks followed behind them, still singing the team fight song and breaking out into hurrahs at every opportunity.[1]

The streets of Cincinnati were filled with adoring crowds that cheered the Red Stockings as their colorful caravan passed on by. Women waved crimson scarves, and red streamers cascaded down from the upper stories of buildings all along the parade route. Cincinnati was clearly in love with its Red Stockings.

The procession ended at the Gibson House. Inside, the Red Stocking players made a brief appearance on the hotel balconies, which set off another round of wild cheers for them, and then the players had lunch and rested up for that afternoon's contest against a local Picked Nine.

About an hour before the start of the 3:00 P.M. game, the Red Stockings emerged from the Gibson House and once again boarded their carriages for the mile-long trek to the Union Grounds. The Streets all along the way were still clogged with cheery cranks, and as the club made its way inside the grounds, Currie's Zouave Band broke out into "Home Sweet Home."

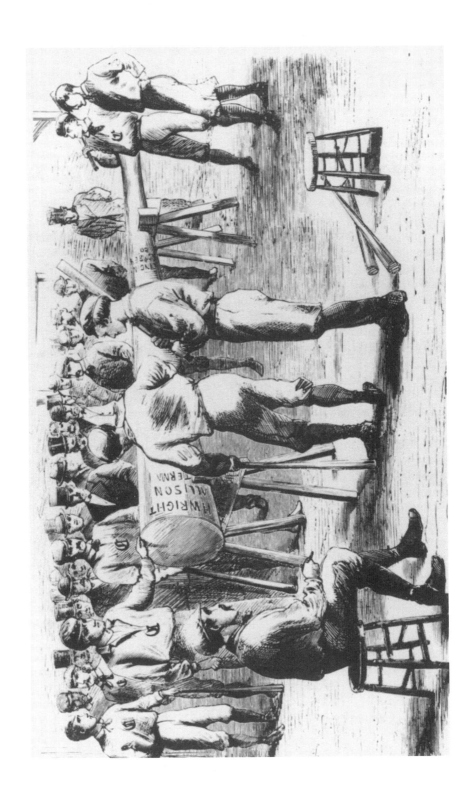

Before the contest began, the Cincinnati Lumber Company made a special presentation to Harry Wright and his players. The lumber company presented the Cincinnati nine with a twenty-seven-foot bat in commemoration of their being "the heaviest batters in the country." The Goliath-sized club read "CHAMPION BAT" on its side, and underneath were listed the names of all of the Red Stocking players.[2] The behemoth bat weighed some 1,600 pounds.[3]

That afternoon the local heroes toyed with the Picked Nine, romping 53–11, as both Wright brothers clouted a pair of roundtrippers and the dubiously Picked Nine committed thirty-one errors.

That evening at the Gibson House, the entire city of Cincinnati came out to fete their beloved baseballers. Tickets to the hardball soiree sold out at five dollars apiece. An enormous red and white "WELCOME HOME, RED STOCKINGS" banner greeted the players and club officials upon their arrival at the hotel. Inside the banquet hall, wreaths bedecked the wall — one for each of the wins on the East Coast tour. The rest of the room similarly dripped with celebratory flowers, flags, and bunting.[4]

A banquet was held in honor of the club, complete with a large pyramid-shaped cake decorated with the names of all the Red Stocking players. Each of the Red Stockings received a bouquet of flowers and a small square of blue silk with his name and position printed on it in gold.

After dinner, every prominent politician, businessman, and judge in the city paraded to the dais to toast the club and tell how much the team meant to the city of Cincinnati.[5]

The final speaker of the evening was Aaron Champion. He peered out over the enormous crowd and said, "Someone asked me today whom I would rather be, President Grant or President Champion of the Cincinnati Base Ball Club." Glancing at his ballplayers seated at the long banquet table beside him, Champion continued with flair. "I immediately answered him that I would by far rather be President of the Base Ball Club!" The crowd roared its approval and broke out into the team fight song, and Currie's Zouave Band played long into the night, finally ending the memorable festivities with a rousing rendition of "Auld Lang Syne."[6] The *Cincinnati Gazette* called the event "one of the most elegant ever seen in Cincinnati."[7]

The following afternoon the bleary-eyed Red Stocking nine jousted with the visiting Olympic BBC from Washington, whom the Red Stockings had defeated the previous week in the Nation's capitol.

It was the Red Stockings' first home game in over a month, and a large and friendly throng of close to 5,000 local cranks showed up at the Union

Opposite: The Red Stockings were presented a twenty-seven-foot-long bat by the Cincinnati Lumber Company, in commemoration of their being "the heaviest batters in the country" (NATIONAL BASEBALL LIBRARY, COOPERSTOWN, N.Y.).

Grounds to spur the club on to victory. Aaron Champion — no fool he — capitalized on the club's newfound popularity by jacking the price of admission from twenty-five to fifty cents for the game. The ticket inflation made no difference to the Queen City fans, who still packed the grounds.

Harry Wright's nine had become a genuine curiosity in Cincinnati, and many people who had never witnessed a baseball game before suddenly appeared at the ballyard, interested in the new, all-professional squad. One old-timer, interviewed on the subject, commented: "I don't know anything about base ball ... but it does me good to see those fellows. They've done something to add to the glory of our city." An associate added, "Glory, they've advertised the city — advertised us, sir, and helped our business, sir."[8]

The Red Stockings, while still a little punchy from the festivities of the night before, nonetheless had enough in reserve to manhandle the Olympic visitors by a score of 25–14.

The city of Cincinnati was alive with the happy, noisy sounds of firecrackers and Zouave bands on the fifth of July as the locals celebrated Independence Day a day late, since July 4 had fallen on a Sunday and the Sabbath still was strictly observed. There also was a strict prohibition against any Sunday baseball at this time, which meant that the Red Stockings were able to take a bit of a break before their July 5 game against the same Olympics.

At the Union Grounds on that afternoon, local dignitaries made patriotic speeches before the game and young street urchins lit off more firecrackers and tried to sneak into the park without paying admission. In the contest, as Currie's Zouave Band serenaded the sun-bleached crowd between innings, the Olympic club stormed to a 4–1 lead after one inning, and for a moment it appeared as if the Red Stockings were gagging on their home cooking. The Cincinnati bats sprang to life in the second frame, however, as the Carmine Hose plated a dozen runs en route to a 32–10 trouncing of the Washington club — the third time in two weeks that the Red Stockings had torched the Olympics. After enjoying the Red Stockings' victory, the happy Queen City crowd headed back downtown for the evening's fireworks display at the Fifth Street Market.

Harry Wright and his troops repacked their bags on Saturday, July 10, for a one-day trek to Rockford, Illinois, to battle the Forest City BBC of that City. The Forest City nine were led by Albert Spalding, the renowned grocery-clerk-turned-pitcher.

It promised to be a tough contest for Cincinnati. Spalding was considered by many to be the top hurler in the game, and Harry Wright feared that the Forest City chucker would be the man who stopped the Stockings' streak.

The prospect of facing the legendary Albert Spalding so terrified Harry's mates that they could manage to score only thirteen runs in their first at-bat. George Wright led off with a prodigious circuit clout, which was followed by doubles by Charlie Gould and Fred Waterman, a single by Doug Allison, a double by Harry Wright, a single by Andy Leonard, a double by Asa Brainard, and a single by Charlie Sweasy, all before even a single out was made. Fred Waterman led off the third inning with a homer, and Brainard, Sweasy, and George Wright all struck four-bag blows in the fourth inning. Charlie Sweasy administered the final shot to the shellshocked Forest City crew with his second roundtripper of the game in the ninth inning, and the free-swinging Stockings pummeled Forest City 34–13, leaving Albert Spalding to long for the relative tranquility of grocery sacking at his market.

The Red Stockings then settled in for a three-week home stand at the Union Grounds. The city of Cincinnati eagerly awaited this part of the 1869 campaign, for the Red Stockings were scheduled to tangle with their local rivals, the Buckeyes, on July 22. While the club prepared to joust with the Buckeyes, *Frank Leslie's Illustrated Newspaper* published a full-page layout lauding the Stockings for their magnificent play that season — a sure sign that word of the sterling nine now had spread all across the land.

The Red Stockings–Buckeyes showdown was the talk of the steamy river city in the days leading up to it. The Red Stockings, given their outstanding success over the course of the '69 campaign, had established themselves as the clear fan favorite in the city, yet many believed that the underdog Buckeyes — given their contempt for all things Red Stocking — would be fired up enough to smear the first stain across the Red Stockings' record that season.

Shopkeepers, wholesalers, open-air marketers, and the rest of the local business trade closed for the afternoon on July 22, and the entire citizenry of Cincinnati flocked to the Union Grounds for the showdown to establish bragging rights in the Queen City. The Red Stockings stepped up to bat in the first inning and posted seven quick runs on the scoreboard, paced by homers by Andy Leonard and Charlie Sweasy. The Buckeyes, barely flinching, responded with five tallies of their own when they took their first licks of the tilt. The Red Stockings, however, had one of the most potent offensive forces of any team in the NABBP — as symbolized by their prized twenty-seven-foot bat for being the "heaviest batters in the country" — and it was foolish to try to match Harry Wright's clobbers *mano a mano* over a nine-inning slugfest. As evidence of this, the red-legged pros went out and pounded the sphere around the Union Grounds to the tune of another eleven runs in the second inning of the contest against the Buckeyes. The Buckeyes responded with four runs of their own to cut the Red Stocking lead to 18–9 after two, but already it was evident that the Buckeyes did not have the power to stand toe-to-toe with the Red Stocking lumbermen for very long.

The Red Stockings plated another ten men in the third, and in the fourth laid waste to the beleaguered Buckeyes with a twenty-three run assault. Every Red Stocking striker batted three times in the fourth inning. Charlie Gould rapped three hits in the single frame, as did Cal McVey, who laced two doubles and a triple and scored all three times. Andy Leonard also cracked three hits — a single, a triple, and a home run — which meant that the ace left fielder just missed hitting for the cycle — in a single inning of play!

In the fifth, the Stockings continued the murderous assault with another twenty tallies. Eighth-place striker Sweasy launched his third circuit clout in five innings of work and, with the score standing at Red Stockings 71, Buckeyes 15, the home plate umpire stepped in and waved off any more bloodshed by the battered Buckeye boys. There was no question now as to which club ruled the Queen City, and the victorious Red Stockings went out after the one-sided contest and celebrated their impressive triumph, while the bloodied Buckeye nine went home to nurse their hardball wounds.

14. Unblemished Still

Basking in the glow of their position as kings of the Queen City, the Red Stockings played host on Saturday afternoon, July 24, to Albert Spalding and the Forest City Base Ball Club at the Union Grounds. Spalding, undeterred by the 34-run bashing he suffered at the hands of the Red Stockings two weeks prior, again took to the pitcher's point for the Forest City nine, seeking redemption.

Cincinnati jumped out to a 3–0 lead in the second, but Forest City countered with four of their own over the next two innings, keyed by a Spalding double, to retake the lead at 4–3. The contest seesawed back and forth over the middle frames as Cincinnati surged ahead 8–4, only to see Spalding and company fight back with three tallies of their own in the fifth to cut it to 8–7.

Going into the eighth inning, the Red Stockings clung to a 12–9 lead, but Forest City stormed back again with another five runs — paced by a key run-scoring single by Spalding — to snatch back a 14–12 lead. The Red Stockings did not score in the bottom of the eighth, and Harry right himself held Forest City at bay in the top of the ninth. As the bottom of the ninth inning began, the Red Stockings were facing defeat for the first time all season.

Replacement James Fowler — who had been placed in the lineup that day when Doug Allison had to rush home to Philadelphia to care for his ailing mother — quickly made the first out of the inning, but then Harry Wright and Andy Leonard cracked successive singles.

Standing on third base, Harry Wright suddenly signaled over to Leonard at first. A short moment later, both of them took off from their respective bases. A double steal! Harry scored to make it a 14–13 contest, and Leonard stood on second — the tying run.

Asa Brainard was up next. As Asa twirled his bat, the Forest City catcher, Bob "The Magnet" Addy, hardly lived up to his nickname as he let a passed ball squirt by him. Andy Leonard scored all the way from second base, and now the contest was tied. The heretofore nervous Cincinnati crowd now erupted with delight, while Albert Spalding stomped around the pitcher's point. The momentum clearly now belonged to the Red Stockings.

Asa Brainard stayed at bat and cracked a double to left field as the cranks hollered forth their approval. Charlie Sweasy was up next. He called out his pitch selection to Spalding, who heaved in a hard one. Sweasy swung mightily and cracked a sharp grounder into left field, past the dive of Forest City shortstop Ross Barnes. Basehit! Asa Brainard wheeled around third base like a runaway train and lumbered home with the 15th — and winning — run. Confetti littered the Union Grounds field as the joyous Queen City cranks celebrated the stirring, come-from-behind win. The Red Stockings had escaped — barely — with their record still unblemished.

As the dog days of August blanketed the Midwest with a wilting heat, the sons of Harry Wright embarked on a three-game mini-tour of the heartland. The first stop was in Milwaukee, where the Red menace whipped the Cream City BBC 85–7 before 3,000 cranks in a massacre halted after seven innings. The rampaging Red Stockings scored in every inning, including outbursts of fifteen, sixteen and nineteen runs. In the nineteenth-run sixth inning, nineteen straight Red Stocking strikers reached base before a single out was recorded. Asa Brainard was the winning pitcher and star striker that day in Suds City, as he cracked eleven hits, scored ten runs, and stole a pair of bags, in addition to getting the "W" for his pitching prowess. Brainard established himself as a two-dimensional hardball threat fifty years before Babe Ruth would gain fame as both a great pitcher and home run hitter.

Stopping next in Illinois, the crimson-hosed hardballers staged a pair of matches against the same Albert Spalding-led Forest City nine they had already bested on two occasions that season. Cranks and reporters from across the Midwest flocked to Chicago for the first of the two contests, held at Ogden Park on the shores of Lake Michigan.

Ogden Park was hardly a hardball palace. The few stands there were rickety and offered a lousy view of the game at hand. The field itself was barely above the level of a sandpit. The fences were so close that anything hit over them was ruled a double instead of a home run. With the mighty Red Stockings coming to town, the game's promoters decided to build additional grandstand seating for the expected overflow crowd, and on the afternoon of the game, as some 10,000 Windy City cranks packed the park, the new stands suddenly collapsed, sending cranks flying everywhere. The suddenly displaced fans had to move to space along the foul lines.[1]

Given the extreme proximity of the cranks to the field, interference became a problem in the contest between Cincinnati and Forest City. Cranks frequently ran onto the field and interfered with balls in play, sending the game into a state of disarray. Undeterred, however, the Wright men still managed to lay into the offerings of Albert Spalding with startling ease, and lit up the country's highest paid grocery clerk to the tune of fifty-three runs in a sloppy 53–32 victory.

Two days later, this time at the far nicer Forest City Grounds in Rockford, Albert Spalding and Asa Brainard met yet again, and once more the Cincinnatians cruised to a 28–7 laugher in the Land of Lincoln. "When the boys of the Forest City Base Ball Club meet any other than the nine red-legged giants gathered from the four quarters of the Union and rendezvoused at Cincinnati, they can gobble them up; but when they run against these nine scarlet runners they come in contact with nine gentlemen whom they cannot handle," reported the *Winnebago County Chief* about the rout in Rockford.[2]

The Red Stockings then returned to Cincinnati for three weeks in the middle of August. At home, the club discovered that some Queen City shops were selling sheet music for "The Red Stocking Scottische," a little ditty in tribute to the sensational nine but dedicated "to the ladies of Cincinnati." On the cover of the sheet music were copies of all of the players' likenesses, which originally had been published in *Frank Leslie's Illustrated Newspaper* a month earlier.

Returning to their home Union Grounds, Harry Wright & Co. continued their winning ways. They pummeled the Central City Base Ball Club of Syracuse — the same club whose field was being used for a pigeon shoot back in June — in back-to-back contests, 37–9 and 36–22, with the second game marred by dispute.

The Red Stockings were shorthanded for the 36–22 victory. Asa Brainard was out with one of his famous phantom illnesses, likely brought on by a little pregame "warm-up" at one of the local taverns, and Doug Allison also was shelved in order to allow his mangled, split-open hands to heal some.[3] As a result, Harry Wright had to add juggler to his many other roles on the club. Harry himself took to the pitcher's point for the contest, and he tapped Fred Waterman to catch, moved Doug Allison to right field to give his hands a bit of a break, switched Cal McVey to center field, and penciled in substitute James Bradford to handle the hot corner for the afternoon.

In the top of the eighth inning of the rematch, with the score knotted at 22–22, Cincinnati erupted for thirteen runs to open a wide lead. By now it was early evening in the Queen City. Dusk was settling in, and the long shadows were making it more difficult to see the ball in play. With the Red Stockings still batting in the eighth, the Syracuse nine began to stall. Under the rules of the NABBP, if a game could not continue due to darkness, then the score would revert back to what it was at the end of the last complete inning. In this situation, it meant that Syracuse could escape with a 22–22 tie with the Red Stockings, which really was as impressive as any victory could be in that season.[4]

The Red Stockings had not made a single out during the thirteen-run eruption, but then all of a sudden Harry Wright struck out. It was the first — and as it turned out only — time in the season that Harry whiffed. The Central

City players howled, claiming that the Cincinnati captain had intentionally K'd in order to speed the game along, so that the eighth inning could be completed and the Red Stockings could go home victorious, instead of merely tied. Umpire Joe Doyle settled the Syracuse nine down momentarily, and Andy Leonard and James Bradford then both struck safeties to account for another run, and for a moment the Syracuse contingent calmed down. Charlie Sweasy then reached base when the Central City third baseman intentionally threw the ball wide to first base on a grounder hit to him, in an attempt to keep the inning going.

Cal McVey was up next, and as he stood at the plate, the controversy exploded anew as the Syracuse club president ordered his club to leave the field, claiming that McVey was going to strike out intentionally just as Harry Wright had done, in an attempt to hurry the frame along. Besides, the Syracuse prez argued, it was too dark out to continue to play, and the Central City players risked injury by having to toil in such dusky conditions. Umpire Doyle dissented and ordered Syracuse back onto the field. They refused his order, so Doyle called the proceedings and awarded the game to the Red Stockings as 36–22 victors.[5]

One of the true highlights of the season occurred on August 11, when Asa Brainard shut out the Riverside BBC, 40–0, on four hits. Shutout games were extremely rare in this era — consider the fact that the Red Stockings themselves were averaging over 40 runs a contest — and Cincinnati's star hurler was toasted throughout the Queen City the night after he whitewashed the Riverside crew.

The Brooklyn Eckfords were in the middle of a midwestern tour when they invaded the Union Grounds on Monday, August 16, but they fell by the wayside like all the other comers. The Red tide swept them under, 45–16, as George Wright, Andy Leonard, and Charlie Sweasy each clouted a pair of homers.

A week later the Southern Base Ball Club of New Orleans visited the Union Grounds, the first team from south of the Mason-Dixon line ever to tour up north. The Southern BBC was best known for its unique brand of footwear: the club sported high-top moccasins without any sort of spikes underneath. Baseball was still a relatively new phenomenon in the South. It had evolved mainly from Confederate prisoners learning to play the game at Union prison grounds during the Civil War. When the war was over, the freed prisoners took the new game back home with them and taught it to their fellow townsfolk.

The Red Stockings used the contest to dazzle the hometown cranks with another unique double play. With Southern pitcher Keefe leading off first base, left fielder Holtzman was at bat and lifted a short liner toward Andy Leonard in left. Keefe, thinking that the ball was going to drop in for a single,

bolted toward second base. Leonard raced in, though, and snared the speedily sinking sphere as Keefe skidded in his tracks and hightailed it back to first.
Leonard heaved the ball to Charlie Gould at first base, but his throw was low.
The Bushel Basket, however, lived up to his nickname and gracefully gathered up the short-hop throw for a rare 7–3 twin-killing, as the Big Easy nine
look on with wide-eyed amazement.

15. "A Most Contemptible Trick"

The game between the Red Stockings and the Union Base Ball Club of Lansingburgh, New York — also known as the Troy Haymakers — on Thursday, August 26, was steeped in wild controversy.

The Haymakers were owned by John Morrissey, a corrupt New York congressman who regularly consorted with gamblers and rigged the outcome of games in which his club was involved. Morrissey, who also was a former boxing champion and owned gaming houses and the racetrack in Saratoga, New York, allegedly had trained his ball club to lose at his command. On this occasion, Morrissey reportedly had wagered $17,000 that the Red Stockings would not defeat his Haymakers.[1]

Damon Rice, grandson of nineteenth-century ballplayer Fletcher "The Bird" Rice, alleged that his grandfather was recruited by John Morrissey to offer a bribe to one of the Red Stocking players in order to assure that Cincinnati did not win the contest.[2]

Fletcher Rice allegedly camped out in the crowded Gibson House lobby a few days before the fabled match and first attempted to bribe the game's umpire, John Brockway — who had played for the Buckeyes — to rig the contest. Brockway was outraged at this bold attempt to sway his judgment, and he threatened to knock the stuffing out of Rice if he did not leave the hotel immediately. Brockway added that, as a result of Rice's bribery offer, all close calls in the contest would be ruled in favor of the Red Stockings.[3]

Having failed to sway the angry arbiter, Rice next sought out pitcher Asa Brainard, on the theory that the hurler was the player who most controlled the outcome of the game. Rice allegedly went to a hotel where Brainard was staying, and had a bellboy deliver a note to the pitcher's room that read, "In one hour you will receive $200. Also instructions for earning an additional $300." Brainard supposedly opened the envelope, read the note, and went back into his room without saying a word. An hour later the bellboy returned to the hurler's room with another envelope containing $200, and another note that read, "If 'Haymakers' score ten or more runs in first and second innings, you get $300 regardless of outcome." This time, Brainard allegedly took the envelope into the room without opening it, said nothing to the bellboy, and closed the door.[4]

There was electricity in the air at the Union Grounds on that Thursday afternoon in late August. Cincinnati streetcars were running extra routes to the Grounds to handle the transports of the city's cranks, and the streets around the field were packed with a multitude of trolley cars, wagons, and coaches delivering fans to the much-anticipated contest. Western Union had installed a special line specifically to transmit game updates to cranks across the city and the country.

Two thousand extra seats were set up at the Union Grounds to accommodate the overflow crowd — estimated at 12,000 total — expected for the battle. The Grand Duchess was packed to capacity, and dozens of horse-drawn wagons and carriages lined the perimeter of the outfield. The Haymakers, despite their seedy reputation, still were considered a top-notch ball club, and many believed that the Red Stockings would have their hands full with the Troy troupe that afternoon. Hundreds of gamblers and oddsmakers were spotted in the crowd, which was the norm for any match featuring the crooked Haymaker club.[5] Many of the gamesters at the Union Grounds taunted the Red Stockings upon their arrival at the field, shouting, "You're gonna get whipped!" and firing clumps of dirt and rotting vegetables at the Cincinnati players.

The game began suspiciously enough in the top of the first inning with the Red Stockings losing the coin flip and having to bat first. The Haymakers, for reasons unknown to the unsuspecting Cincinnati crowd, elected to put their ace pitcher, Cherokee Fisher — who had pitched for the Buckeyes of Cincinnati the season prior — at second base for the contest, and started the inferior Charlie Bearman on the pitcher's point. Bearman, though, was up to the task initially, and shut out the Red Stockings in the top of the first.[6]

In the bottom half of the inaugural inning, the Haymakers scored a half-dozen runs off Asa Brainard, including four tallies with two outs, to take a 6–0 lead. Fly balls dropped by Waterman, McVey, and Leonard all contributed to the quick six-run deficit.

In the top of the second, Cincinnati stormed back with ten runs of their own, including six that occurred after two men were out. It was apparent at this juncture that umpire Brockway indeed was leaning toward the Red Stockings on anything close. On one play, Brockway called a Cincinnati baserunner safe at home when it appeared to almost everyone else that he clearly was out. It would have been the third out of the inning. Instead, the Red nine rallied for another half-dozen scores in the frame.

In the bottom of the second, the Haymakers plated another seven runners to retake the lead at 13–10. Once again, the Red Stocking defense was underwhelming, as Andy Leonard dropped another fly ball, Doug Allison let a passed ball slip by him, and the usually surehanded George Wright muffed one grounder and unleashed one wide throw to first base. The thirteen runs scored by the Haymakers over the game's first two innings would have satisfied the terms of the alleged offer made by Fletcher Rice to Asa Brainard.

In the top of the third, Fred Waterman clouted a two-run homer to cut the Troy lead to 13–12, and an inning later a run-scoring two-bagger by Charlie Sweasy knotted the seesaw contest at 13–13.

In the top of the fifth frame, Cincinnati burst ahead 17–13. Another controversial call by Brockway marred the inning and set the stage for later shenanigans in the game. In the top of the fifth, as the Red Stockings rallied, George Wright stole second base. The Haymakers went ballistic when Brockway called George safe at second, and Troy captain Bill Craver roared at Brockway to reverse the call, but to no avail. At that moment, Haymaker president John McKeon ran onto the field from his perch at the scorer's table and, while waving his rattan cane menacingly in the air, hollered at Brockway that if he made any further controversial calls against the Haymakers, then McKeon would pull his club off the field.

In the bottom of the fifth, the Haymakers scored four runs, paced by a two-run homer by left fielder Steve King, to retie the score at 17–17.

The top of the sixth inning was the most controversial frame of the entire 1869 season for the Red Stockings. Cal McVey strode to the plate and fouled an offering down between the feet of Haymaker catcher Craver. Under 1869 NABBP rules, if the catcher caught a foul tip on the first bounce, the striker was out. Craver scooped up the sphere on the third hop, shoved the ball under Brockway's nose, and claimed that he had snared it on the first bounce, so that McVey should be out. Brockway laughed at Craver's feeble effort to steal an out. "It bounced three times!" Brockway hollered back at Craver. "McVey's not out!"

Craver continued to protest. "You're blind as a bat!" he screamed at Brockway with his eyes ablaze and the veins in his neck protruding. "You've been calling plays against the Haymakers ever since the damn game began!"[7]

As Craver continued to bellow, John McKeon again burst forth from the scorer's table and stormed onto the field. McKeon told his club to clear the field and stack their bats. Hoots and jeers cascaded down upon the Haymakers as they began to lug their equipment off the field. Aaron Champion and Harry Wright, meanwhile, implored McKeon to keep playing, and even offered to use a substitute umpire for the remainder of the contest. McKeon refused every offer. Umpire Brockway then climbed up on a chair and announced to the crowd that the game was over because the Haymakers had refused to continue, and the Red Stockings were declared the victors.

The Queen City crowd cheered Brockway's decision, but quickly turned on the Haymakers as the club headed toward its large coach. The angry Cincinnati fandom began to bombard the crooked Haymaker nine with fruit, vegetables, bottles, rocks, and pieces of sod. The Troy squad frantically piled into the horse-drawn omnibus to escape the wrathful mob, and they were chased back to their hotel by several irate Red Stocking cranks. All the while, as chaos reigned supreme on the Queen City grounds, Cal McVey stood at the plate like a lonely sentinel, waiting to resume his at-bat.

As it turned out later, l'affaire Craver had been staged. John Morrissey had directed his catcher to concoct such a scene when the score was tied, so that the Troy owner and his band of cronies could collect their winnings by having prevented the Red Stockings from winning the contest.

While umpire Brockway had awarded the game to the Red Stockings by forfeit after the Haymakers had left the field, and even went so far as to enter his decision in the Red Stockings' favor in the club's scorebook, the NABBP would later overrule the umpire. After the season ended, at the December 1869 NABBP convention, a motion was made to add twenty runs to the Red Stockings' total for the game, which would have erased the tie and would have given Cincinnati a 37–17 victory. The NABBP Judiciary Committee, however, tabled the motion, and the tie score remained intact — the first blemish on the Red Stockings' 1869 record.[8]

The city of Cincinnati howled at the injustice of it all after the contest had ended in such a premature way. The *Cincinnati Gazette* lambasted the Haymakers for their "most contemptible trick to wrest from the Red Stockings a complete victory ... no measures were too disgraceful for their backers to attempt in order to win their money."[9]

The Buckeyes, who were scheduled to meet the Haymakers in a game on the day after the Red Stocking contest, immediately canceled the match, stating that they refused to be seen on the same field as the unscrupulous Haymakers. The Cincinnati Base Ball Club met and discussed withholding the Haymakers' portion of the gate until the Troy club apologized for its disgraceful behavior, which the Haymaker hippodromers indeed did do, after the season had ended.[10]

16. 103 to 8!

Harry Wright & Co. ended the month of August with a bang, in an incredible 103–8 vaporization of the rival Buckeyes at the Union Grounds on August 31.

One hundred and three to eight! In a perverse irony, the contest actually was a benefit game for the Buckeyes to boost their coffers. Benefit indeed.

The game — and the word is used loosely here — lasted only eight innings, and the Red Stockings notched double-digit attacks in five of the frames, including a pair of twenty-run-plus outbursts. The Stockings clouted eleven home runs in the slaughter, including two each by Allison, Leonard, Sweasy, and George Wright, and one apiece by Gould, McVey, and Harry Wright. The sadsack Buckeyes missed nine flies on the afternoon — including a half-dozen drops by right fielder McKitrick — and also muffed another ten balls on the ground. The bombed-out Buckeye hurler for the afternoon was named Black, and his mood surely fit his moniker after the eight-inning annihilation.

The Red Stockings led 37–1 after three innings of play, but this was just a preview of what lay ahead. In the fourth, the mighty Cincinnati batmen struck for twenty-six runs, twenty of which scored before even the first out was made. Fred Waterman led off innocently enough with a single and stole second. Doug Allison doubled in Waterman. Harry Wright clouted a two-run homer. Andy Leonard doubled. Asa Brainard reached on a three-base error as Leonard trotted home. Charlie Sweasy singled in Brainard. Sweasy swiped second base and scored on a Cal McVey safety. George Wright doubled in McVey. Charlie Gould reached on an error by the beleaguered Black, allowing Wright to score. Waterman batted for the second time in the inning and cracked his second single. Allison rapped his second two-bagger of the inning, scoring Gould. Harry Wright reached on a two-run error. Leonard singled. Brainard's safety plated Wright and Leonard. Sweasy doubled in Brainard, McVey doubled in Sweasy, and George Wright doubled in McVey. Wright then swiped third base — as if it was necessary at this point — and scored when Gould cracked a base hit. Waterman laced his third hit of the incredible inning, a double that plated Gould. Allison and Harry Wright both singled before Andy Leonard finally made the first out of the inning. Every

Hurley, Sub.; G. Wright, S. S.; Allison, C.; McVey, R. F.; Leonard, L. F.
Sweasy, 2d B.; Waterman, 3d B.; H. Wright, C. F.; Brainard, P.; Gould 1st B.

ED STOCKING B. B. CLUB OF CINCINNATI.

The 1869 Red Stocking baseball card issued by the Peck & Snyder Sporting Goods store in New York (NATIONAL BASEBALL LIBRARY, COOPERSTOWN, N.Y.).

Red Stocking striker notched at least one hit in the bountiful frame, and each Red Stocking scored at least twice. Waterman, Allison, and Sweasy all cracked three hits in the inning to lead the charge of the Wright brigade.

In the sixth, the hit fest continued as the Red Stockings mugged Black to the tune of another twenty-one runs. In this frame, the first nineteen Red Stocking strikers reached base and eighteen runs scored before a single out was recorded.

As the days began to grow shorter and crisper, the Red Stocking juggernaut rolled on. On the morning of September 10, 1869, the Cincinnati Red Stockings stood alone atop the baseball world with a record of 49 wins, no losses, and one controversial tie. The scarlet-hosed bashers had scored 1,676 runs to their opponents' 485 up to that point in the '69 campaign, which computes to an average victory margin of 39–11.[1]

It was time again, though, for the sons of the Queen City to pack their bags, but this time the train that pulled out of the Indianapolis and Cincinnati station headed westward. Harry Wright and his hardy troupe of hardballers were taking their act first to Missouri, and then all the way to California.

17. The California Tour

The Red Stockings headed out of Cincinnati on September 14, bound for St. Louis, the first stop on their westward journey. Harry Wright brought along another substitute for the tour, a seventeen-year-old infielder named Oak Taylor, who previously had seen duty with the Great Western and Walnut Hill clubs in Cincinnati. As the club boarded the train at the Indianapolis and Cincinnati station, a young lady gave each of the players a tiny set of red stockings that they could pin to their lapels. Most of the players wore the miniature red hose throughout the western swing.

The wooden Pullman cars on which the team traveled featured a three-tiered, first-class sleeping compartment illuminated by whale oil lamps.[1] The cars also featured spacious sitting and smoking rooms, which were considered major attractions on a long tour such as that upon which the Red Stockings were about to embark.[2] But even given this degree of nineteenth-century luxury inside the train, the ride itself still was often hair-raising. *Cincinnati Commercial* writer Harry Millar, along for the western tour, remembered how the cars zigzagged so much that it was impossible to stand erect while on board. The cars also jumped the track on occasion, which made several of the players nervous. Their nerves were further shot as they roared out West and viewed wrecks of other locomotives that had jumped the tracks and had been left for scrap at the scene of the accident.[3]

The sons of the Queen City disembarked in St. Louis for a tilt with the Union Base Ball Club at the Union Ball Grounds in the Gateway City.

In front of some 3,000 cranks curious to see the now-famous Red Stockings, Harry Wright's nine bombed the Unions for eighteen runs in the first inning and ten more in the second on the way to a 70–9 rout. Both of the Wright brothers cracked a pair of homers in the one-sided contest. The *St. Louis Democrat* raved about the Cincinnati club's "clockwork fielding and steam-powered batting."[4]

The Red Stockings also won the following day's match in St. Louis against the Empire BBC, 31–14, and then reboarded the rails, bound for California. The Cincinnatians rode over the historic Union Pacific and Central Pacific tracks that — four months earlier on May 10, 1869 — had been joined at Promontory Point, Utah, to form the first transcontinental rail route in the nation's history.

Through the rugged mountain ranges of Colorado and Utah and across the arid desert lands of Nevada and California, the scarlet-legged journeymen rode, ready to showcase baseball excellence to the cranks in the Golden State. The Pacific rail lines would play a major role in introducing the game of baseball to Westerners, just as the Civil War had been responsible for presenting the pastime to Southerners a few years prior.

As the Red Stocking traveling party rode across the Western countryside, many of the players gawked at their first sights of — to them — such exotic creatures as antelope, buffalo, bison, deer, and even prairie dogs. Harry Wright and a few of his mates who carried guns even took shots at the animals as their train roared across the tracks, but the players' shooting prowess — particularly from a zigzagging train — hardly matched the rifle-armed accuracy that they always exhibited on the playing field.[5]

There was another reason why several of the Red Stockings packed heat on the trip out West: the very real threat of Indian attacks all along the way. At the same time that the Red Stockings were traveling across the nation's first transcontinental link, the newspapers were filled with stories about Indian attacks in Montana, Nebraska, and Kansas, and the U.S. Army had sent General George Custer, among others, out West to try to quell the terror. George Wright, fifty years later in 1919 at the famous Black Sox World Series, would captivate his neighbors in the box seats at Crosley Field in Cincinnati with gripping tales of how he and his fellow Red Stockings slept with their pistols under their pillows on the train ride out West, fearful of a Sioux attack, but ready for a showdown with the Indians if necessary.[6]

Harry Wright and his men wound up making it to California without any Indian trouble, and they rolled into the Golden State on Saturday, September 25, and took a steamship down the Pacific Coast and into San Francisco Harbor. At the wharf, the club was greeted by John Durkee, the president of the San Francisco Association of Base Ball Clubs, a welcoming committee delegation, and another 2,000 San Francisco cranks eager to catch a first glimpse of the now-famous-across-the-land Cincinnati Red Stockings. From the wharf, the Stockings were escorted in six fancy carriages to the downtown Cosmopolitan Hotel. All along the route to the hotel, even more San Franciscans strained to get a look at Harry Wright and his celebrated nine.[7]

The Red Stockings' West Coast tour was of course major news in the San Francisco area newspapers. A large advertisement in the *Daily Alta California* trumpeted the news of the arrival of the club in the city:

RECREATION GROUNDS.

SATURDAY . . . . SEPTEMBER 25

RED STOCKINGS

AND

EAGLES

THIS GREAT MATCH COMMENCES AT 1 O'CLOCK.

SEATS HAVE BEEN ERECTED FOR 1,000 PERSONS IN THE PAVILION,

WHICH WILL BE STRICTLY RESERVED FOR LADIES AND THEIR ESCORTS.

ADMISSION . . . . ONE DOLLAR

"No club in the United States, nor, in fact, all the clubs put together, have done so much toward creating a furor for base ball and making it so pre-eminently a national pastime as the Red Stockings," the *San Francisco Chronicle* stated.[8]

On that first brisk, windswept autumn afternoon in the City by the Bay, the Red Stockings were to meet the Eagles, who were the Pacific Coast champions, and who sported their own perfect — albeit far less game-intensive — record of five wins and no losses for the 1869 campaign.

The *Daily Alta California* provided its readership with exhaustive coverage of the Red Stockings' stay in San Francisco, and appeared to be awestruck by the presence of such diamond gods in their fair burg. The *Daily Alta* previewed the California matchups by stating:

> The Red Stockings, it is said, will open the eyes of those who have considered themselves 'base-ball sharps,' as they make the game so much superior to the old style, that they bear the same relation as chess and chequers. And as to throwing 'swift balls,' they are said to get the ball so quickly to second base, that their opponents cannot make an average of one run in an inning.... It was through [Harry Wright's] constant exertions that the nine have proved to be so strong. It is true that nearly all the players were first-class ballists before they joined the Cincinnati Club, but the credit of their being nurtured and carefully trained, so as to work together in a faultless manner, solely falls to the steady head-work of Captain Wright.[9]

The streets leading to the Recreation Grounds at Folsom and Twenty-fifth Streets were clogged with carriages, wagons, and carts as San Franciscans clamored to see the red-legged wonder of the Midwest in action. Adding to the congestion were streetcars that continuously arrived from the downtown area with more carloads of cranks eager to see the Red Stockings at play by the bay. Extra service was provided by the Omnibus Railroad Company from the Metropolitan Hotel on Montgomery Street to the Recreation Grounds, with a new coach departing every five minutes.

The *San Francisco Chronicle*, not to be outdone by its journalistic competitors in the Bay Area, complimented the Red Stockings on their sense of fashion and physique: "It is easy to see why they adopted the Red Stocking style of dress which shows their calves in all their magnitude and rotundity.

Everyone of them has a large and well-turned leg and everyone of them knows how to use it."[10]

Harry Wright & Co. proved to be ungracious — though stylish — guests that first afternoon as they bombed the Eagles, 35–4. Cincinnati plated a dozen runs in the first inning alone, with ten runs scored before even a single out was made. The most amazing part of the frame was that George Wright, Charlie Gould, and Charlie Sweasy all stole home plate. The Queen City squad tormented the Eagle battery of Miller and Calvert all afternoon as they wheeled around the bases and swiped home plate a grand total of seven times. Larcenous left fielder Leonard personally was responsible for three of the heists, and Cincinnati ran away with the contest — literally.

The *Daily Alta California* was aghast at the mismatch:

> [Eagles' hurler] Miller pitches very good balls for California clubs, but they just suited the Red Stockings, who batted his swift balls with the greatest of ease. The principal difference between the two Clubs is in their Pitchers: While the Red Stockings advance the leg, at the same time they brought the arm forward, and thus gave to the ball the impetus of the whole body and leg; the Eagle Pitchers remained firm in their position, with the legs spread, and having barely the force of the body from the waist to impel the ball. The Red Stockings have adopted the new style of pitching, while the Eagles still cling to the old rule of remaining firm in their position while delivering the ball.[11]

Concerning Cincinnati's unstoppable base thievery, the *Daily Alta* observed: "The Red Stockings, among other things, excel our clubs in their agility upon their legs. Their manner of escaping from first to second base excited applause, and the style should be copied by the Eagles.... Before the pitcher's arm was drawn all the way back they started for the second base, and the swiftest ball a catcher could throw could not overtake them. The Eagles, on the other hand, dilly-dallied around their first until too late, and seldom made their second, except when a ball was sent away out in the field."[12]

The *San Francisco Chronicle* particularly lauded George Wright for his derring-do on the basepaths: "[He is] full of capers ... [hopping] about like a kitten on his base — now touching it with his hands, again with his feet, then falling across it with his body."[13]

The *Daily Alta*, however, saw fit to credit the battered Eagle nine for one modest accomplishment — the fact that they kept the score to *only* 35–4: "The Eagles, though their score shows small, deserve great credit for keeping down to a moderate figure the number of runs made by the Red Stockings; in other matches with clubs in the East and West they have made 103 runs.... It must be remembered that the first nine of the Red Stockings are picked men from among the best players of the United States, are in constant practice, and have perfected a system of telegraphic signals as easily recognized as if spoken words were used."[14]

That evening, after the conclusion of the inaugural San Francisco tilt, the Red Stocking and Eagle players ventured out to the Alhambra Theater to see the play, "The Field of the Cloth of Gold."[15]

After taking the Sabbath off, the Red men returned to the Recreation Grounds and roughed up the Eagle BBC for the second straight game, 58–4, behind a sparkling five-hit masterpiece by Asa Brainard on the pitcher's point. Brainard also swatted a home run, one of six launched by the Carmine Crew on an afternoon in which brisk bay breezes blew dirt, sand, paper, and other assorted debris across the grounds, and the Red Stocking players held fast onto their white jockey-style caps before the blustery wind blew them away.

The *Daily Alta*:

> The Red Stockings have arranged a set of orders so brief that frequently only the name of the player is called and he hastens to do what is requisite; an instance of their alacrity and perfect understanding was given ... [when] a sky-ball was sent between shortstop and right field, for which either might have gone, but the Captain called 'McVey,' and the right fielder at once put himself in position to catch it, but the Captain also called 'Wright' in the same breath, and the shortstop ran and dropped on his knee under McVey's hands, so that if missed by the first it could still be caught before reaching the ground.[16]

The following afternoon, the Cincinnati baseballers took a breather from their diamond duties and engaged in a cricket match against the California Eleven. The Red Stockings, featuring cricket stalwarts such as George and Harry Wright, emerged victorious, 118–79, as George made a grand total of 53 runs.[17]

It had become plainly evident that there was no competition in the Bay Area that could come close to matching the Red Stockings. With each succeeding contest, the mismatches got progressively worse. On September 29, the Red Stockings plastered the Pacific Base Ball Club 66–4 on a typically bright, frigid, windswept afternoon in San Francisco. Andy Leonard clouted a trio of roundtrippers, including a grand slam. Concerning Leonard's four-run four-bagger, the *Daily Alta* enthused,

> The confidence of the Red Stockings in their striking was shown when Andy Leonard went to the bat with a man on each of the three bases, and every probability that one or more would be put out when the ball would go to the field, but the striker carefully measured the ground with his eye and sent the ball whizzing along the grass out past right field and over the graveled outside walk, enabling every man on a base to get safely home and the striker himself to make a home run. It was a very effective strike, scoring four runs for the Red Stockings.[18]

The beat went on a day later when the Pacifics were pasted, 54–5. George

Wright swatted four homers through a fierce gust that kicked up small sand-storms throughout the blustery contest. Harry Wright pitched for the Red Stockings that afternoon, and Asa Brainard patrolled center field. Doug Allison also got a break from his backstop duties as Harry Wright moved him to third base for the contest and had Fred Waterman man home plate. By now the *Daily Alta* was referring to the Red Stockings as "the invincible club," and the paper also groused about the San Francisco nines' impotent offensive capabilities against Cincinnati pitching. "The slow 'twisters' sent by Harry Wright bothered [the Pacifics] as much as the 'chain lightnings' delivered by Asa Brainard," the newspaper moaned.[19]

The Red Stockings wreaked total hardball havoc on October 1 when they ravaged the Atlantic BBC, 76–5. The Cincinnati strongmen clubbed fourteen homers in the contest, which incredibly lasted only five innings. Every player in the Red Stocking lineup, save Andy Leonard, homered at least once; Sweasy and Waterman bashed three apiece. George Wright clouted a pair of roundtrippers in the massacre, which gave the star Cincinnati shortstop a total of ten home runs in five games over the course of the California trip. The Red Stockings, as a team, had cracked forty-one circuit clouts over the five-game stretch in San Francisco. The *San Francisco Chronicle* noted that Fred Waterman "generally hit the ball which is the hardest for the fielders to stop. He takes the ball upon the end of the bat and sends it whizzing through the air about four inches off the ground, making what is called a 'daisy cutter.'"[20]

The most eye-popping part of this tilt, though, was the fourth inning, in which Harry Wright's crew scored forty runs. Forty runs in one inning! Forty-three Cincinnati strikers marched to the plate in the historic frame as the Red Stockings set a season record for single-inning run productivity. Charlie Sweasy led the murderous assault with five hits in five at-bats and five runs scored — in a single inning. The Cincinnati second sacker cracked two singles, a double, a triple, and a homer in his five plate appearances, meaning that he hit for the cycle in a single frame. George Wright also notched five hits in the incredible inning, including a homer and three triples. McVey and Brainard each lashed a quartet of safeties in the never-ending frame. The Atlantic hurler that afternoon — who surely set some sort of record for pitching ineptitude — was named Lennon, and he was a fool on the hill that day, to be sure. The *San Francisco Chronicle*, showing something of a flair for black humor, published the box score of the rout at the end of a daily feature entitled "Suicides Yesterday."[21]

Faced with no real competition in the Bay Area, the Red Stockings decided to stage an exhibition among themselves for the entertainment of the competition-starved San Francisco cranks. The "Harry Wrights," led by the Wright brothers, Waterman, Leonard, McVey, and four other San Francisco players, defeated the "Asa Brainards," featuring Brainard, Gould, Allison, Sweasy, and a quintet of other Bay Area ballists, 20–7, as Harry Wright bested Asa Brainard on the pitcher's point in the most closely contested match on the California tour.

After a final 46–14 drubbing of a San Francisco Picked Nine club, the Red Stockings packed their equipment and prepared for the next leg of the western tour in Sacramento. Before departing from San Francisco, however, Harry Wright's men were guests of honor at a gala farewell banquet in the Pacific Hall at the California Theater in the city, as hosted by the players from the Eagle, Pacific, and Atlantic nines. Players from the California clubs toasted the mighty Red Stockings. Some of the salutes to the Cincinnati nine were touching, while others were humorous. One San Francisco player lauded the Red Stockings by declaring, "May they never meet the wash in which they may be bleached." Another player joked, "Our National Game: may we never think it Wright to let our exertions in its support come to a short stop." Harry Wright and Aaron Champion then spoke on behalf of the club, and everyone raised a glass of cheer — although Wright and Champion made sure that none of their nine did any excessive celebrating. "[The Red Stockings] were magnificently entertained by over fifty of their hosts," the *Daily Alta* reported. "There was a pleasant interchange of sentiments of satisfaction and pleasure on the part of the entertained and entertainers. Toasts, speeches, and songs, after dinner, kept the party together until after one o'clock [in the] morning."[22]

San Francisco and the *Daily Alta* finally bid the Red legs adieu, with the paper lauding how "our visitors must be commended for the urbanity they have exhibited under all circumstances; not a single instance of exulting over their opponents, carping at the play of each other, nor disapproval at the decision of the umpire — everything being received as a matter of course. This conduct has won for them the esteem of all with whom they have come in contact, and their late competitors are particularly enthusiastic in their praise."[23] It was no wonder then that ten years later Harry Wright would write to a friend in San Francisco and state, "My recollections of [the] former visit to your city are still vivid and the trip is remembered as one of the pleasantest and most enjoyable in all my experience."[24]

The Red Stockings traveled on the Central Pacific to Sacramento, and the Crimson Hose staged another match against a Picked Nine club consisting of both Sacramento and San Francisco ballplayers at the Agricultural Park in the state's capital, and the Red tide rolled again, 50–6.

The Red Stockings then rode the new transcontinental route back east through Nevada and Utah. At Promontory Point they switched lines for the next leg of the trip, which would take them up to Omaha. While on a layover in Cheyenne, George Wright and Oak Taylor got off of the train to visit a nearby shop and look at moss agates, which the pair had been collecting on the western tour. As the forty-five-minute layover ended, the engineer blew the train's whistle and the conductor hollered, "All aboard!" Wright and Taylor, however, were nowhere to be found. Aaron Champion and Harry Wright panicked, wondering about the whereabouts of their star shortstop and prize substitute. Champion raced to tell the conductor to hold the train while Harry jumped off the train to search for the wayward duo. Quickly enough, Harry ran into his brother and Taylor, and the three of them beat a hasty retreat back to the train, with Harry's linen duster flying from behind. The rest of the Red Stocking players still on board doubled over with laughter at the sight of their captain, their superstar, and their substitute all sprinting back toward the train as other passengers yelled at them to hurry up and stop delaying the trip. The incident made for some great joshing for the rest of the trip to Nebraska.[25]

In Omaha, the sons of Cincinnati — still laughing over the Wright and Taylor caper in Cheyenne — routed that city's nine 65–1, as Harry Wright pitched and scattered just four hits. The contest provided quite a juxtaposition with regard to the cranks on hand at the game. The Red Stockings were honored to play the match in front of Ulysses S. Grant's vice president, Schuyler Colfax, who was in the area to visit Army outposts and inspect railroads. But, on the other hand, midway through the game the Red Stocking players heard a couple of dogs growling and noticed a commotion in the stands. As it turned out, many of the cranks in attendance had gotten bored by watching the rout on the field, and had decided to stage a dogfight between the two canines instead, hoping for something a little more competitive to watch. Aaron Champion noticed that more people seemed to be interested in the pugilistic pooches than in his ball club, and quickly informed the umpire that the Red Stockings would stack their bats and leave the grounds unless order was reinstated in the stands. The dogfight was broken up, the pooches were sent packing, and everyone turned their attention back to the blowout on the field.[26]

Harry Wright chucked his second four-hitter in as many days as he stuffed the Otoes of Nebraska City the next afternoon, 56–3. The Wright brothers, in that contest, combined for fifteen hits and fourteen runs scored between them.

After a 51–7 rout of the Occidental BBC in Quincy, IL, the Red Stockings ended their western swing with a tilt against the Marion Base Ball Club in Indianapolis. The game was played on a chilly, overcast October afternoon, and many of the Red Stocking players kept their overcoats on between innings to stay warm. Back-to-back steals of home in the second inning by Fred Waterman and Doug Allison paced the Cincinnatians to a 63–4 laugher as Harry Wright hurled his third four-hit gem in four games.

That marked the end of the western swing. The Red Stockings had remained undefeated over the course of a dozen surprisingly easy matches against clearly inferior Western clubs. The roving hardballers had traveled by stagecoach, steamboat, and locomotive, and had cast aside all comers. The club also had netted $1,000 on the tour, which put wide smiles on the faces of Harry Wright and Aaron Champion.[27] Now, however, as had been the case in early July at the conclusion of the East Coast swing, it was time for the scarlet-hosed sons of Cincinnati to return home to the adoration of the Queen City.

18. "Veni! Vidi!! Vici!!!"

There was another tumultuous reception for the returning hardball heroes at the Cincinnati train station late in the evening on October 16. While the numbers may not have matched those who greeted the club upon its return from the East Coast tour earlier in the season, nonetheless Harry Wright and his mates were mobbed by hundreds of delirious cranks once again, and Currie's Zouave Band saluted the undefeated warriors with versions of "Hail to the Chief" and "Home, Sweet Home." From the station, the Red Stockings traveled in coaches to the Gibson House for a late-evening, welcome-home dinner.

In their first taste of home cooking in over a month, the Red Stockings met the Philadelphia Athletics at the Union Grounds on October 18 in a match advertised by the club as the "last grand game of the season." Cincinnati cranks again had to reach a little deeper into their pockets to pay for tickets to the contest, as Aaron Champion once again jacked the admission price for the game from twenty-five to fifty cents. Nonetheless, the Union Grounds stands were filled with close to 6,000 fans as game time drew near on that blustery afternoon in the Queen City. In the match, George Wright whacked a pair of home runs to pace the Red Stockings to a 17–12 victory as cranks shivered under blankets in the Union Grounds stands.

The baseball season of 1869 stretched longer than it does today. Even though the game against the Athletics had been advertised as the "last grand game of the season," as October became November and Ohioans braced for another long winter, Harry Wright's hardy hardballers still were tearing up the turf at the Union ballyard and elsewhere.

On November 3, Harry Wright's boys of winter trekked to Louisville for a match with the Kentucky Base Ball Club. Asa Brainard never even made it onto the steamboat that carried the club from Cincinnati to Louisville, and as the contest began at the Bluegrassers' old Kentucky home, the Cedar Hill Grounds, the Red Stockings could only field a team of eight men. As a result, Harry Wright pitched, Andy Leonard and Cal McVey were left to patrol the entire outfield, and Charlie Sweasy and George Wright played a far deeper infield than they normally would. Even given their shorthandedness, the Red Stockings still coasted, 58–9, as Charlie Gould, Fred Waterman, and Doug

Allison — the second, third, and fourth-spot strikers in the mighty Cincy lineup — combined for twenty-one hits, twenty-five runs scored, nineteen runs batted in, and seventeen stolen bases in the Louisville slugfest, which was halted after five innings due to darkness — both of the sky and of any chance of a comeback by Kentucky in this rout.

After a 40–10 blasting of a Louisville Picked Nine squad the following afternoon, the Red Stockings returned home to Cincinnati for a November 6 contest with the New York Mutuals, the same squad that the Wright men had trimmed 4–2 on June 15, in the single most important victory of the season for the Cincinnatians. Because the days were growing shorter now the starting time for the tilt was moved up from 3:00 P.M. to 1:00 P.M. Some 7,000 cranks donned extra clothing and heavy coats and flocked to the Union Grounds for the truly final game of the 1869 season.

On that gray and blustery November afternoon, as the citizenry prepared to settle in for the long hard winter ahead, the Cincinnati Red Stockings completed their unconquered campaign with a 17–8 triumph over Boss Tweed's Mutuals. George Wright and Charlie Gould homered in the season finale. "The closing game for the Season of 1869," Harry Wright penned in his scorebook, and then he gloriously added, "Veni! Vidi!! Vici!!!"[1] — invoking the triumphant battle cry of Julius Caesar at Zela.

That evening, Gibson House proprietor A. G. Corre hosted an end-of-season farewell banquet for the undefeated Red Stocking nine. The party rivaled the July gala in terms of jubilation and fanfare. Each Red Stocking player received a $50 bonus in tribute to the unbeaten season. It was a coronation for the hardball kings from the Queen City.

The Red Stockings had finished their incredible season without a single loss. A debate commenced, though, regarding the proper number of victories to attribute to the historic nine. Harry Wright, in his scorebook, listed the Red Stockings' record as 56 wins, with one tie — the lone blemish being the controversial draw with the Haymakers on August 26. Harry, however, counted only victories against other NABBP clubs in his tally, and did not include any of his squad's wins against Picked Nine ball clubs, which he considered to be patchwork teams put together on a temporary basis. Wright did, however, include all games against other NABBP clubs even if they lasted less than nine innings. On several occasions over the course of the season, the Red Stockings would be leading in a game by several dozen runs in the middle innings when the tilt would be halted due to rain or darkness or the necessity of the team leaving to catch a train or a steamship to another city. In each of these instances, even though the match lasted less than nine innings, there was no chance of the outgunned opponent ever staging a successful comeback, and as long as the bare minimum of five innings was met, then the game was included in the victory column by Captain Wright.[2]

While Harry listed 56 victories, the *Cincinnati Commercial* reported the Red Stockings' record as 57–0–0, the *Cincinnati Enquirer* tallied 58 wins, and the *New York Daily Tribune* awarded the Carmine Hose 61 victories in 61 contests. Each of these three newspapers apparently had its own hardball philosophy regarding what constituted a victory but, interestingly enough, each tabloid saw fit to award the Red Stockings a victory for the disputed Haymaker game. Ironically, it appears that Harry Wright himself was the only one who considered the Haymaker match a tie — recall how even the umpire, John Brockway, awarded the contest to the Red Stockings and even made such a notation in the scorebook — while the rest of the baseball world recognized the seedy affair as a bona fide Cincy victory, albeit by forfeit.[3]

Perhaps the best appraisal with respect to the Red Stockings' record for 1869 would be 60 wins with no losses. This figure is reached by acknowledging the 56 victories over other NABBP clubs, then adding the Haymaker contest as another victory by forfeit, and then also including the three wins against the Picked Nine clubs of San Francisco, Sacramento, and Louisville — clubs that certainly were trounced by Cincinnati's original Big Red Machine, but that nonetheless were more talented than several of the NABBP nines. Thus, the best evaluation of the Red Stockings' 1869 record may be 60 wins, without any other blemishes.[4]

It is quite likely that Harry Wright and his men would have thought very little over any debate concerning the proper number of victories with which to credit them. Rather, the Red Stockings would have been satisfied with a single sentence penned by esteemed baseball writer Henry Chadwick in the *New York Clipper* shortly after the season ended. Chadwick wrote, "The result of the season's play places the Cincinnati club ahead of all competition, and we hail them as the champion club of the United States." That was precisely what Aaron Champion and Harry Wright had strived for when they were putting the game's first all-professional club together a year earlier.

The Cincinnati Red Stockings played in front of approximately 200,000 cranks during the 1869 campaign, traveling some 12,000 miles. The Red legs scored 2,396 runs and gave up only 574, for an average victory margin of 40–10.[5] The Carmine Clouters bashed 169 home runs over the course of the season, an average of close to three a contest. George Wright led the roundtripper parade with 49 clouts. Charlie Sweasy was runner-up with 30, while Andy Leonard cracked 23, Charlie Gould 21, Fred Waterman and Doug Allison 11 apiece, Cal McVey 10, Harry Wright 9, and Asa Brainard 5.[6]

George Wright was the Red Stockings' unofficial Most Valuable Player. In addition to his 49 homers, the brilliant shortstop whacked 304 hits in 480 at-bats for an eye-popping batting average of .633. Wright also scored 339 runs. This is the equivalent of a modern-day slugger averaging a home run, five hits, and five runs scored in every game.[7]

Albert Spalding, the great Forest City pitcher, later wrote about the Red Stockings that their undefeated season "demonstrated at once and for all time the superiority of an organization of ball players, chosen and trained and paid for the work they were engaged to do, over any and all organizations brought together as amateurs."[8]

The 1869 Cincinnati Red Stockings, in addition to being recognized as the first all-professional club, also deserve commendation for having showcased baseball from coast to coast. The Red Stockings were like missionaries of the diamond, spreading the hardball gospel from Boston to San Francisco and everywhere in between. Youngsters would go to the Union Grounds and other ballyards and watch the sensational Cincinnatians at play, and then the youngsters would go home and imitate the manner and style of the unbeaten, spike-shod ambassadors. Harry Wright's men were not just hired-gun professionals, but also were pioneers and teachers of the burgeoning game.

Cincinnati journalist Harry Ellard penned the following ode to the unbeaten 1869 Red Stockings:

THE REDS OF SIXTY-NINE

An old man sat in his easy-chair
    Smoking his pipe of clay,
Thinking of years when he was young,
    Thus whiling his hours away.

Thinking when he was but a boy,
    So full of mirth and glee,
And we hear him say: "How things have changed;
    They are not as they used to be.

"When I was young, and played baseball
    With the Reds of Sixty-nine,
We then knew how to play the game;
    We all were right in line.

"We used no mattress on our hands,
    No cage upon our face;
We stood right up and caught the ball
    With courage and with grace.

"And when our bats would fan the air
    You bet we'd make a hit;
The ball would fly two hundred yards
    Before it ever lit.

"A home run all could easily make,
    And sometimes six or eight;
Each player knew his business then
    As he stepped up to the plate.

"Let's see! There's Leonard and George Wright,
   And Sweasy and McVey,
With Brainard and Fred Waterman —
   These men knew how to play.

"'Doug' Allison, too, could bat in style,
   And so could Charlie Gould,
While Harry Wright oft said with pride,
   'My boys are never fooled.'

"The game you see them play to-day
   Is tame as it can be;
You never hear of scores like ours —
   A hundred and nine to three.

"Well, well, my boy, those days are gone;
   No club will ever shine
Like the one which never knew defeat,
   The Reds of Sixty-nine."

19. 1870: Improving on Perfection

After the 1869 season, the Red Stockings published a souvenir pamphlet that detailed the glory of their unbeaten campaign. "Our Red Stockings" was the title of the ode to the magnificent nine. "The grand and unequalled success of our world-renowned and incomparable Cincinnati or 'Red Stocking' base ball club is fresh in the memory of the sporting fraternity," the monography marveled. "Their triumphant march from the Atlantic to the Pacific during the past summer and the great deeds in their line performed, astonished thousands of admirers of the national game at the time."[1]

The 1869 Red Stockings earned gate receipts totaling $29,726.26, and disbursed $29,724.87 in salaries and related expenses, leaving a grand profit of $1.39.[2] The denizens of the Queen City, however, cared not a whit about the Red Stockings' balance sheet. They simply were in love with their ball club and the fame that it brought to their fair burg. It likewise mattered little to the Cincinnati cranks that Charlie Gould was the only native talent on the supersquad. A player's birthplace immediately was forgotten once he donned the white flannel jersey sporting a scarlet Old English "C" on its front.

Over the winter of 1869–70, as club members ice-skated across the flooded-over Union Grounds, Harry Wright was faced with the unusual task of trying to improve upon an undefeated ball club. The first item of business involved salary increases. Harry jacked his and his brother George's wages up to $2,500 for the 1870 campaign, while the rest of the Red Stockings jumped up into the $1,500–$2,000 bracket. The Red Stockings very nearly lost Charlie Sweasy to the New York Mutuals during the off-season. "We came very near losing Sweasy," Harry Wright wrote to baseball writer Henry Chadwick, "but he acted like a man and, although sorely tempted, resolved to stand by his contract. I shall always think a great deal of Sweasy for acting the way he did," Harry concluded.[3]

The success of the '69 Red Stockings, though, had spawned competitors. The *New York Times* published a list of eighteen clubs that it called "patrons of the professional system," and the *Times* also chronicled each nine's method of payment, such as whether the team paid by salary like the Red Stockings, or only shared gate money, or "appointed to office" its ballplayers. The *Times* listed the Red Stockings, the Brooklyn Atlantics, the New York Mutuals, and the Philadelphia Athletics as "the four leading professional clubs of the country."[4]

The *New York Times* article also mentioned the rise of another squad, the new "$10,000 nine" of the Chicago White Stocking Club.[5] Citizens of Chicago were outraged that Cincinnati — or "Porkopolis," as Chicagoans preferred to call it — could lay claim to a superior ball club. As a result, Windy City denizens raised $20,000 to attract a powerhouse squadron and meet all salary and expense demands. The Chicago White Stocking club even went so far as to publish an advertisement in the *New York Clipper* seeking spike-shod talent. The advertisement read: "On the 12th of October, 1869, was organized in Chicago, the Chicago Base Ball Club, having for its object the employment of a picked nine composed of first class professional ball players.... The undersigned hereby calls the attention of base ball players to the subject. All professionals desirous of connecting themselves with the Chicago Club are requested to address, stating terms as to salary, etc. and with full understanding that all communications will be held as strictly confidential."[6]

A *Chicago Tribune* editorial fueled the hardball fervor in the Windy City, demanding "an organization as great as [Chicago's] enterprise and wealth, one that will not allow the second-rate clubs of every village in the Northwest to carry away the honors in baseball."[7] Indeed, clubs now were gunning for the sons of Cincinnati.

The irony of the Chicago White Stockings' quest was that a year earlier Chicago had been one of the most vocal cities in opposition to the Red Stockings' plan to turn all-professional. Many Chicago scribes denounced the Cincinnati plan to bring in out-of-towners to play for pay, suggesting that Harry Wright's recruits were nothing more than a gang of hired gunslingers brought in to lead the fight against all invading hardball desperadoes. When the White Stockings decided to go professional, however, it was deemed a worthy civic endeavor. A Windy City pedigree was no longer even a requirement. The *Chicago Post* even poked fun at the idea of restricting the White Stocking Club to Chicago citizens, chortling the "of course the players will all be Chicago men; although just now they are all 'visiting' other parts of the world. These gentlemen are to be invited to come 'home,' and are to be paid a sufficient sum to make the invitation effective. Chicago ... has got the material for the best ball club in the world. Just now that material is a little 'scattered.'"[8] What was good for the Red Stockings was now good for the White Stockings.

Spring flooding in 1870 caused significant damage to the Union Grounds, and Aaron Champion and Harry Wright scrambled to make speedy repairs to the soggy grounds so that the Red Stockings could engage in preseason workouts.

The club warmed up for the 1870 season with a 34–5 win over a Picked

Nine before only 400 cranks at the Union Grounds on Monday, April 18. The Red Stockings then packed their gear and followed the Ohio River down to Louisville. The time had come to see whether Harry Wright's nine were mere one-year wonders or a true hardball dynasty.

In Louisville, the Red Stockings picked up right where they had left off in 1869. They dusted off their war clubs and bludgeoned the Louisville Eagles 94–7, at Cedar Hill Park. The Cincinnati sluggers pounded out twenty-nine runs in the eighth inning and — probably just for insurance — then plated another twenty-three in the ninth. Doug Allison wound up with ten hits on the assaultive afternoon, including one in every inning save the second. Charlie Sweasy cracked the first Red Stocking homer of the season, a three-run clout in the twenty-nine-run eighth-inning uprising. Cal McVey, in his usual ninth spot in the striking order, lashed nine hits and scored a dozen tallies. The Wright brothers could have beaten the Louisville crew all by themselves. Harry pitched all nine innings and also cracked nine hits — including eight singles — plus he scored a half-dozen runs and swiped a half-dozen bags, including heists of home in the second and ninth innings. George, not to be outdone by his older brother, laced eight safeties himself, scored a dozen runs, and poached an incredible eight bases. He also swiped home plate in the ninth inning. The concept of stealing home plate when your club is up by more than eighty runs fairly boggles the mind.

Harry Wright's traveling band next picked up its stakes and trekked southward for a six-day, six-game run in New Orleans. The Red Stockings' trip to the Big Easy basically was a precursor to today's spring training ritual of limbering up in a warmer climate before settling in for the summer at home up north.

The Red Stockings were not exactly greeted with open arms in the Crescent City. Five years after the end of the Civil War, New Orleans still was occupied by federal troops as it struggled to rebuild itself during the period of Reconstruction. Most of the city's fine old homes lay in ruins as a result of the war, and trade and industry had almost totally been halted. The economy of the shattered South was in complete collapse, and New Orleans was no exception. As a result, many in the city despised the Red Stockings if only for the fact that they came from Ohio, a free state and Union stronghold during the war.

Undeterred, the visiting Cincinnatians opened in New Orleans on April 25 at the Louisiana Base Ball Park, where they stuffed the New Orleans Pelicans 51–1 as Asa Brainard hurled a six-hitter and Cal McVey went six-for-nine and hit for the cycle.

The northern nine continued their assault the following afternoon with an 80–6 thrashing of the Southern Base Ball Club. In the game's third inning, the Stockings struck for twenty-eight runs as twenty-seven strikers reached base before the Southern squad registered even a single putout. Doug Allison was a one-man wrecking crew on the afternoon, lashing ten hits in thirteen plate appearances, including six singles, two doubles, a triple, and a home run as he matched Cal McVey's cycle feat of the day before.

The following afternoon, a Gulf Coast storm pelted the city, forcing cancellation of the match between the Red Stockings and the Robert E. Lee Base Ball Club. There are no reports that the legendary Civil War general was in town for the match between the Red Stockings and his namesake club, but given the results of the first two contests in New Orleans, it is likely that these Robert E. Lees were better off avoiding any battle with the scarlet-legged northern forces commanded by Capt. Harry Wright.

The following afternoon it stopped raining just long enough for the Red Stockings to squeeze in a game with the Atlantic Base Ball Club, although the field was a veritable quagmire of mud and water and the clubs were forced to move the location of homeplate and all three bases so that strikers would have a reasonably dry area in which to hit. The rest of the saturated grounds were dotted with mounds of sawdust that, while somewhat absorbent, made things still more messy in the long run. Even under such dank conditions, the Red Stockings still prevailed with ease, 39–6.

The sons of Harry Wright also waltzed over New Orleans' Lone Star BBC, 26–7, and then also finally waged hardball war against the Robert E. Lees in the final battle of New Orleans. With new substitute Ed Atwater pitching, Capt. Wright's flannel-clad forces repelled Lee's troops by a 24–4 margin. After the Lee skirmish, the Red Stockings discovered that not all members of New Orleans society despised them. A group of area ministers approached Harry Wright and his men and, on behalf of the local Christian community, thanked the Red Stockings for abstaining from playing Sunday baseball while in the city — despite several financially tempting offers to do so. The men of the cloth remarked to Harry Wright that they truly appreciated the fine example set forth by the Red Stockings, who were not so mammon-driven as to violate the Sabbath in the Cresent City. It was a refreshing change, the clergymen concluded, from the usual merchants-in-the-temple attitude that many other northern clubs had exhibited when visiting the city.[9]

Leaving Louisiana, the Red Stockings steamboated up the mighty Mississippi to Memphis for a tilt with the city's Oriental BBC at the Memphis Driving Park. In a frightful demolition, the ravaging Red Stockings obliterated the Orientals 100–2 in a match halted after six frames for reasons of darkness and mercy. It had to be disheartening for a team to be down 26–0 before it even took its first licks at the plate, but that was precisely the situation in which the Memphis crew found itself after only a half inning of play. After three innings it was already 59–0 and Fred Waterman and Asa Brainard already had belted seven hits apiece. The onslaught continued for another three frames, and when the Red Stockings cracked the centennial mark, the white flag was raised by the hapless hometowners.

Returning to the Queen City, the Red routers dumped the Forest City BBC in a pair of matches, 12–2 and 24–10. On May 20, substitute Ed Atwater was given the pitching nod as the carmine-clad clouters crushed the amateur College Hill BBC 72–10 in a match played in a small wooded park a few miles to the north of downtown Cincinnati. George Wright and Charlie Sweasy particularly shone in the contest. Wright lashed nine safeties, scored nine runs, and swiped eight bases, including home plate in three consecutive innings, while Sweasy duplicated the nine-hit, eight-stolen bases feat, but could only manage to pilfer home in two consecutive frames.

If five steals of home in a 72–10 blowout would appear to be showing off, well, there was a reason for it on that sunny springtime afternoon. Twenty girls from a nearby college were at the game, and after the contest the Red Stockings and their female fans adjourned to the nearby residence of a certain Professor Wilson for lunch and conversation. "No over-persuasion was required," the Cincinnati Commercial reported about the invitation extended by the girls to the Red Stockings, "for the boys were gallanted by the young ladies to the tables." In order to ensure that the proper decorum was maintained during the luncheon, a dour Mrs. Judge Miller was called upon to chaperone the entire affair, and the civilized Stockings socialized without incident, although apparently it took some doing for Harry Wright to convince his boys to leave their bevy of female admirers at the end of the day.[10]

George Wright must have been greatly reinvigorated by his afternoon with the girls, for the following afternoon he belted five home runs in a 42–17 rout over the Amateur BBC at the Union Grounds. The sterling shortstop connected for three circuit clouts in his first three at-bats in the ballgame, all of which occurred in the game's first two innings.

Four days later, the Red Stockings took the field against the Union BBC of Urbana, Ohio, and inflicted the most vicious beating they had ever imposed on another nine. The final score on this afternoon was Red Stockings 108, Unions 3. Yes, that's right—108–3. It is very easy to become blasé about frequent bashings administered by Harry Wright's boys. A forty- or fifty-run rout might appear similar to a college football blowout today. Even a sixty- or seventy-run pummeling might not look that different from a college basketball mismatch in the modern era. But 108–3 — it boggles your mind and spins your head clear around.

The sacrificial lamb sent to the pitcher's point slaughter by the Unions that afternoon was named Hagenbuck. There is no record of what his first name was and, frankly, he probably was grateful for a little anonymity after this debacle.

Hagenbuck probably should have realized that it was going to be a rough afternoon when, in the first inning, Harry Wright cracked a line drive right off his shoulder. That's when Hagenbuck made his first mistake of the contest — he elected to stay in the game even though he was writhing in agony.

A twenty-one-run second inning by the Red Stockings did not shake the hardy Hagenbuck. Nor did a seventeen-run third inning — or even a twenty-two-run fourth. But there was no stopping the rampaging Red men this afternoon. They plated another eighteen tallies in the fifth and, at the end of five innings, already led 82–2. With the game barely half over, Charlie Gould already had cracked eleven safeties; Cal McVey, with four singles, four doubles, a triple, and a homer, already had hit for the cycle — after five innings of play. In the sixth inning, Hagenbuck accomplished a small victory of sorts, relatively speaking, by holding the Red Stockings to a mild three-run spasm. The Crimson Clobbers, however, had not an ounce of charity in them on this occasion, and they pounded out another twenty-three tallies over the final three frames of the mind-numbing mismatch.

Seven Cincinnati strikers had ten hits or more on the incredible afternoon. Ironically, a substitute named Dean led the Red Stocking hit parade with fourteen safeties. Dean, McVey, and George Wright all hit for the cycle. Asa Brainard, the slugging pitcher, laced a dozen hits of his own. Andy Leonard got at least one hit in all nine innings played. It's no wonder that Union pitcher Hagenbuck let his first name be lost to the ages, and probably more surprising that he didn't change the whole blasted thing after this hardball humiliation.

And the beat went on. The day after the historic 108–3 vaporization of the Unions, the Red Stockings trekked up the road for a joust with the Dayton BBC. If the Dayton lads thought that Harry's hardballers had slugged themselves all out the day before, well, they faced a rather unpleasant surprise. The amazing Red machine rolled over the hapless Dayton nine, 104–9. The Cincinnati supermen now had plated an unheard of 212 runs over the course of a mere two games.

At the end of May, the Red Stockings packed for another East Coast tour. The trip began on a strange note as the Red Stockings began the journey by traveling to Cleveland. On the way there, the roof of the passenger car ahead of the Red Stockings caught fire, and the passengers from the burning car fled in a panic into the car carrying the ball club. Brakemen on the train quickly contained the fire, but the smoky smell from the burned-out car stayed for the rest of the trip to Cleveland.[11]

Arriving in Cleveland, the Red Stockings were treated to a boat cruise on Lake Erie. While enjoying themselves out on the lake, the boys had dinner and smoked complimentary cigars. The following afternoon, the Red Stockings blasted the Forest Citys 27–13 in front of 3,000 cranks — the largest crowd in Cleveland baseball history to that point.

From Cleveland the Cincinnati nine rode the rails to Rochester, which was the site of the famous 1869 game wherein Harry Wright and his men played groundskeepers and groomed the soggy field after an afternoon downpour had delayed the game. On this occasion, Cincinnati uprooted the Flower City Base Ball Club 56–13. A day later, the Wright men clubbed the Ontario BBC at the Oswego Base Ball Grounds 46–4, and then caught a late-afternoon train for Pittsfield, Massachusetts, for their next contest against the Old Elm Base Ball Club there. In Pittsfield, the Red Stockings arrived to find an enormous banner strung across the town's main street that read, "CINCINNATI." Harry Wright thanked the town's fathers for the unexpected tribute, and then he thanked his club after they chopped the Old Elms down to size by a score of 66–9. A pelting rain halted the Pittsfield contest after seven innings, but Harry and his mates let the brooms and sawdust go untouched this time, since the game was official and the day's gate receipts were safely in their hands.

The Red Stockings then continued their Massachusetts swing by riding the rails east to Boston, where they rolled over the Harvard BBC 46–15 at the Hub's Union Base Ball Grounds. The cranks in the Boston stands were left awestruck by a mammoth eighth-inning blast by George Wright that easily cleared the distant wooden fence at the grounds. As the ball rolled farther and farther away, dozens of Boston street urchins gave chase to it, hoping to land the newly lopsided sphere as a souvenir of the Red Stockings' visit to the Hub.

The Stockings continued their Bay State bombardment with a 17–4 rout of the Lowell BBC nine and a 32–5 sinking of the Clipper BBC. While still playing in Boston on June 9 in a steady drizzle against the Tri-Mountain Base Ball Club, the carmine-hosed clouters romped 30–6, and Andy Leonard matched George Wright's home run prowess with his own prodigious poke out of the Union Base Ball Grounds and into the crooked streets of the Hub. Beantown cranks were aghast at the power of the Monsters of the Midwest.

The Red Stockings then piled into a caravan of stagecoaches and rumbled out to Worcester for a June 10 tilt with the Fairmount BBC at the Worcester Driving Park. Several dozen Worcester cranks crowded the lobby of the hotel where the Red Stockings were staying, desirous of meeting some of the legendary Cincinnati hardballers. Harry Wright and Charlie Gould, resplendent in their crisp Red Stocking flannels, greeted the starstruck cranks and talked baseball with them for a while. A few of the Worcester fans even offered Gould champagne, but he politely refused it.[12]

At the Worcester Driving Park, with ash-colored clouds overhead threatening to unleash a deluge at any moment, the Fairmount nine stormed out to a quick 3–0 lead over the Red Stockings in the first inning of their tilt. Asa

Brainard looked tired and sluggish on the pitcher's point, and may have sampled some of the champagne that his mate Gould had eschewed. The raucous Worcester contingent in the stands lustily cheered its Fairmount nine as they took to the field in the bottom of the first, holding on to a 3–0 lead. This might be the day, the Worcester cranks excitedly muttered to each other, that the mighty Red Stocking juggernaut finally was stopped.

The Fairmounts had struck the first blow in this battle, but then found themselves ducking cannon fire for the rest of the rainy afternoon. The Red Stockings answered the 3–0 deficit with two dozen runs of their own in the bottom of the first, and then ten more in the second and another dozen in the third. The Fairmount nine had tugged on the sleeping lion's tail with their three runs in the first, and the beast had awakened with a mighty roar.

Showers poured down on the mud-soaked clubs as the soggy Stockings continued to pile up runs. By the seventh inning, the Worcester Driving Park grounds would have better served as a fishing hole, and the umpire halted play as the drenched baseballers headed for cover, with the Red Stockings romping 77–19. George Wright, Asa Brainard, and Cal McVey each struck a hit in every inning of the rainy rout.

As showers continued to pelt the city of Worcester that evening, the Red Stockings boarded a locomotive bound for New Haven, Connecticut, where they next were scheduled to battle the Yale BBC. Just as in 1869, though, the tilt was washed out as the rainstorm continued to drench all of New England.

The waterlogged hardballers headed back to the rain-soaked New Haven train station and got on board another locomotive. As the car steamed and belched and pulled out of the city, Harry Wright paused and looked out his dripping window into the showery, black Connecticut night.

It was just like a year earlier, Harry Wright must have thought, when it poured all along the way into New York. The Red Stocking skipper sighed and closed his eyes. He fell asleep hoping that this journey into the Big Apple would be as fruitful as it had been the year before.

20. The Battle of Brooklyn: "Though Beaten, Not Disgraced"

Gotham newspapers already were conceding defeat to the Red Stockings when the Cincinnati nine wheeled into town. The tabloids moaned that the mighty Red legs would "win all the games played, because the New York nines [are] not harmonized."

The opening game of the New York series was on June 13 against the Mutuals. The *New York Herald* blasted the Red Stockings for driving ticket prices for the contests from twenty-five to fifty cents, but Harry Wright shrewdly — and correctly — figured that New York cranks would pay the higher prices to see the much-anticipated games. The size of the crowds at the ball grounds bore him out.

At 3:00 P.M. on the 13th, the Red Stockings pulled up to the Union Grounds ballyard in a large hotel coach drawn by a pair of horses, already dressed for play in their white cricket flannel uniforms and scarlet hosiery.[1] Harry Wright & Co. were loudly cheered by the Big Apple throngs. "It's the Cincinnatis!" cried many cranks in the crowd. "Here come the Red Stockings!" exclaimed many others. Dozens of youngsters clamored around the hardball kings of the Queen City and excitedly followed the club into the grounds.

The lack of any real pregame warmups made no difference, though, as 10,000 cranks watched the Stockings manhandle the Mutuals 16–3 on the drizzly afternoon in Brooklyn. Asa Brainard was indeed an ace on the pitcher's point, giving up just two hits in the contest. It looked as though the ink-stained wretches in the New York press were right on target about Cincinnati's superiority over the local nines.

On Tuesday, June 14, in the twenty-eighth game of the 1870 season, the Red Stockings met the Brooklyn Atlantics at the Capitoline Grounds. The rain from the previous day had ended, and the weather had turned sunny and pleasant in Gotham. At Hudnut's Pharmacy at the corner of Broadway and Ann Street in lower Manhattan, the thermometer read 86 degrees by mid-afternoon.[2]

The Capitoline Grounds comprised the first enclosed baseball park in the history of the pastime, located in what is now the Bedford-Stuyvesant section of Brooklyn. The grounds featured much more than just a ballfield. There were sheds, stables, a restaurant, a bandstand, several sitting rooms on the second floor for the Atlantics' female partisans, plus clubhouses and storage areas on the first floor for use by the competing nines. In the wintertime, the Capitoline Grounds were flooded from a city main and used for skating and, amusingly enough, baseball games played on ice, featuring many of Brooklyn's top players gliding across the basepaths, raising ice shavings instead of dust.[3]

The Atlantics were the pride of the East and the squad that many believed would best be able to slug it out toe-to-toe with the Red Stockings. The Atlantics were nearly as fashionable as the Red Stockings, what with their long navy blue pants and crisp white shirts complete with a large "A" stitched on the front.

An estimated 20,000 Brooklynites shelled out the requisite fifty cents apiece — just as Harry Wright had predicted — to watch the big matchup. Hordes of additional Atlantic cranks concocted schemes to watch the ballgame from other vantage points. The *New York World* reported, "Hundreds who could or would not produce the necessary fifty-cent stamp for admission looked on through cracks in the fence or even climbed boldly to the top, while others were perched in the topmost limbs of the trees or on roofs of surrounding houses."[4]

Harper's Weekly sent a correspondent and an artist to the showdown, giving the game national prominence. In Cincinnati, the usual throng of Red rooters invaded the Gibson House to follow the game via Harry Millar's telegraphic updates.

The Brooklyn lineup featured several standouts from the pastime's primitive era. Dickey Pearce, their shortstop, stood only 5 feet 3 inches, but was considered one of the top infielders in the nineteenth-century game. Pearce also mastered the art of dropping down a "fair-foul hit"; he would bunt the ball down the baseline so that it would start off in fair territory but then twist foul, away from the fielder. Such a ball was considered in play until 1877.

The Atlantics also featured pitcher George "The Charmer" Zettlein, a former sailor who had served under Admiral David G. Farragut, and second baseman Lipman Pike, the first renowned Jewish ballplayer. Pike once raced a standardbred horse for $200 — and won. The incredible race, which covered one hundred yards, featured the horse, named Charlie, starting off twenty-five yards behind Pike. Once the standardbred reached Pike, then the ballplayer took off. Pike and Charlie galloped neck-and-neck for most of the race until the speedy hardballer began to pull away from the horse. Charlie, seemingly realizing his embarrassing role in the annals of equine history, suddenly began to gallop furiously, but to no avail. Pike won the race by four yards.[5]

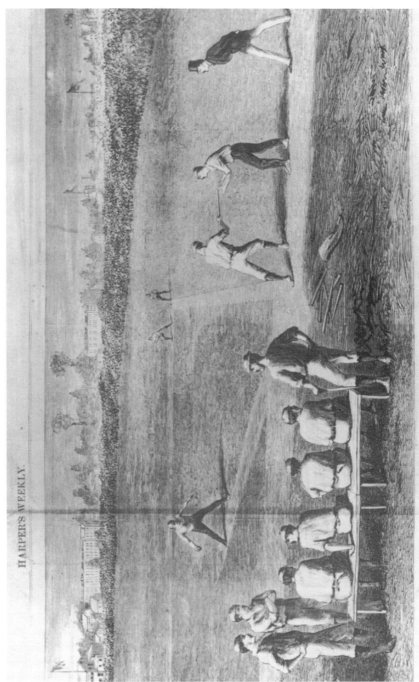

[SEE PAGE 427.]

The captain of the Atlantics was also their catcher, Bob Ferguson, who owned perhaps the greatest nickname in the history of the national pastime; "Death to Flying Things."

Ferguson, however, also appears to have been death to some of his teammates. He was an overbearing individual, full of bluster and rage. Sam Crane, a fellow nineteenth-century ballplayer, once remarked of Ferguson that "turmoil was his middle name, and if he wasn't mixed up prominently in a scrap of some kind nearly every day, he would imagine he had not been of any use to the baseball fraternity and the community in general."[6] On the occasion of the match with the Red Stockings, "Death to Flying Things" was embroiled in a bitter feud with a baseball writer for the *New York Herald*. The scribe had written a column suggesting that Ferguson was driving away his best teammates because of his confrontational attitude, and Ferguson's response to the article was to threaten to punch out the *Herald* writer. As a result, the *Herald* reporter refused to cover the Atlantics-Red Stockings matchup in person, and instead used telegraphed reports of the game with which to write his story.[7]

In the top of the first inning, the Red Stockings sprinted out to a 2–0 lead as Harry Wright singled to drive in brother George and Doug Allison. Two innings later, the scarlet nine made it 3–0 as Fred Waterman singled in George Wright, who had reached base on an error and then had stolen second.

Asa Brainard was toiling on the pitcher's point for Cincinnati, and he mesmerized the Atlantics over the game's first three innings. Brainard was helped by several sparkling defensive plays early on by his crimson-clad mates. Henry Chadwick, who was covering the contest, marveled at how Harry Wright would reposition his fellow fielders for each Atlantic striker. The concept had been unheard of prior to Wright employing it. "In fact," Chadwick later gushed, "Harry Wright would at one time be seen playing almost back of second base, while Sweasy would be nearly a first base fielder, and so they changed about, coming in nearer or going out further, just as they judged the balls would be sent to the different batters. It is the lack of judgment like this that [the Atlantic] outfielders show their inferiority to the skillfully trained Red Stockings."[8]

The Red Stockings must have been reading their own press clippings in

Opposite: Harper's Weekly published this sketch (by C.S. Reinhart) of the June 14, 1870 loss to the Brooklyn Atlantics — the Red Stockings' first loss since October 1, 1868. Compare the Red Stockings' knickers to the Atlantics' full-length trousers, and notice how close to the bags the first and third basemen played, due to the "fair-foul" rule. Also note the thin infield baseline, the lack of dugouts, the catcher standing directly behind the batter, and the umpire clad in top hat and morning coat (NATIONAL BASEBALL LIBRARY, COOPERSTOWN, N.Y.).

the bottom of the fourth frame, though as the Atlantics rallied back with a pair of runs — due mainly to a two-base throwing error by Fred Waterman — to make it a 3–2 ballgame. In the sixth, the Brooklyn nine grabbed the lead as the Red Stockings' vaunted defense disintegrated once again. Harry Wright himself muffed a leadoff fly ball by Dickey Pearce, and then Doug Allison committed a troika of miscues behind the plate, and all of a sudden it was 4–3 in favor of the Atlantics.

In the top of the seventh, as late afternoon shadows blanketed most the Capitoline Grounds lawn, the sons of Cincinnati roared back and recaptured the lead as Brainard and Sweasy singled, moved up a base on a McVey ground-out, and then scampered home when George Wright rapped a sharp single off the tiring "Charmer" Zettlein.

Neither club could hold a lead, it seemed. In the bottom of the eighth, with the sun setting in the Brooklyn borough, the Atlantics clawed back to tie the game. With one out, hot cornerman Charlie Smith cracked a triple over Andy Leonard's head in left field, which caused the Brooklyn cranks to spring to life. "Old Reliable" Joe Start then stepped up to the plate and smacked a hard liner into right field. Cal McVey raced over to make a spectacular snare of the ball, and in one motion fired the ball homeward, where Smith was bearing down on Doug Allison. McVey's peg was perfect, but Allison muffed the ball and Smith scored as the Brooklyn mob roared. The battle was now knotted at 5–5.

Neither club scored in the ninth inning and the Atlantics, after making the final out, gathered their bats and began to leave the field. They had tied the mighty Red Stocking nine, and they were content to leave it at that. "To have played a nine inning game with the famous Red and tied them with so small a score as 5–5 ... seemed the very acme of fame," the *New York Daily Tribune* commented.[9]

Harry Wright, however, howled. Storming in from center field, he bolted over to the umpire, where he was joined by Aaron Champion, and together the two Cincinnatians demanded that the game be continued. The Red Stockings had not been on the losing side of a contest since October 1, 1868, when these same Atlantics had dumped them 31–12.

The umpire, Wright, Champion, and Brooklyn captain Ferguson all jawed for a while, and then the group headed over to where writer Henry Chadwick had been watching the game. Wright made his appeal to the legendary rule-making pioneer of the sport, and pointed out the playing regulation stating that in the case of a tie score at the end of nine innings, the match must continue "unless it be mutually agreed upon by the captains of the two nines to consider the game as drawn."[10] Harry Wright reiterated his demand that play continue, which meant that the Atlantics faced the prospect of losing by forfeit, 9–0, if they stayed in the clubhouse.

The Brooklyn captain, "Death to Flying Things" Ferguson, snorted and snarled. In reality, Ferguson wanted the game to end in a tie. He and his Atlantic mates were paid based upon each game's gate receipts, and Ferguson drooled at the thought of arranging an even more lucrative rematch between the two clubs at the Capitoline Grounds, which would net him and his mates about an extra $300–$400 apiece. Given the pressure exerted by Harry Wright and the Brooklyn crowd to continue play that day, however, Ferguson had no choice but to stomp off and retrieve his reluctant teammates.

A soft twilight settled in over the city as play resumed in the top of the tenth inning. The Red Stockings were stopped cold by George Zettlein, and the Atlantics ran in to their bench, eager to end the Cincinnati unbeaten streak. With one out, Jack McDonald and Dickey Pearce reached base, and suddenly the Red Stocking streak was in jeopardy. The Atlantics' Charlie Smith cockily strode to the plate, confident that he was about to become a local hero. Smith shouted out his pitch selection to the bone-weary Brainard. McDonald danced off second and Pearce bounced off first. Brainard checked the two runners, twirled the grass-stained sphere in his sweaty hand, stepped forward, and fired. Smith swung lustily, but only lifted a meager pop-up in the direction of George Wright at shortstop. McDonald and Pearce stomped back to their respective bags as Wright circled under the spinning fly. Suddenly the crafty shortstop let the ball plop down in front of him. McDonald froze on second. Wright pounced on the sphere and chucked it over to Waterman at third. Waterman stepped on the base to force McDonald, and then heaved the ball over to Sweasy at second for a double play. McDonald and Pearce stood like a couple of cigar store Indians on their respective bags, flabbergasted at what had just occurred before their very eyes. The Red Stockings, meanwhile, whooped it up and ran off the field, having dodged an awfully close bullet. Boisterous boos and jeers cascaded down from the Brooklyn stands, aimed at the wily Wright, and George "was the victim of every name on the rooter's calendar ... but through the atmospheric blue streaks, his white teeth gleamed and glistened in provoking amiability."[11]

The rejuvenated Red Stockings pushed across two runs in the top of the eleventh inning. Brainard doubled to right field and was driven in by Cal McVey, and George Wright knocked home Charlie Sweasy. Now it was 7–5 Cincinnati as the beleaguered Brooklynites trudged in for their final licks. Many in the crowd began to leave the Capitoline Grounds. The Atlantics had staged a valiant battle, but looked to be just a day late and a buck short on this occasion.

Asa Brainard still was hurling for Cincinnati in the bottom of the eleventh. Dusk was settling in across the grimy borough, and the sticky, sooty summer heat had knocked the starch out of the Red Stocking chucker. Charlie

Smith led off for Brooklyn and cracked a single to left field. The remaining crowd cheered hopefully. Brainard was disgusted with himself for having surrendered a leadoff hit, and he eyed Smith as the Atlantic baserunner took a lead off first. Joe Start was up next. He called out his pitch selection, but the weary Brainard fired wildly and the wayward sphere skidded behind Doug Allison. Charlie Smith hotfooted it all the way to third as the Atlantic cranks whooped a little louder now. "Old Reliable" Start then lifted a high fly ball over the head of Cal McVey in right field, and the sphere rolled in among the fringes of the crowd located behind the outfielders.

Many accounts of this game have stated that at this point McVey was jumped by Brooklyn rowdies, kicked at, and seriously roughed up as he fought to retrieve the ball. The *Cincinnati Commercial* railed that "in pushing the crowd aside to get at the ball, McVey was kicked at by a scoundrel." Another report stated that a Brooklyn policeman allegedly pulled out his billy club and whacked one boisterous crank with it, and then dragged him off. The most interesting and relevant account of the controversial play, however, was that of McVey himself. The Red Stocking flychaser, in an interview shortly before his death in 1926, stated that no one ever climbed on his back or seriously interfered with him. According to McVey, he did encounter a degree of difficulty in retrieving the ball, but hardly to the violent extent trumpeted in most reports of the play.[12] In any case, it is clear that there was some minimal degree of interference that prevented McVey from speedily retrieving the ball, and as a result, Smith scored and Start ended up on third base. Now it was 7–6. John Chapman then grounded out to Fred Waterman for the first out, with Start staying on third. Bob Ferguson approached the plate next. "Death to Flying Things" normally batted from the right-hand side of the plate, but Asa Brainard's jaw dropped when he saw Ferguson saunter over to the left-hand side of the dish and call out his pitch selection. It was the first significant instance of switch-hitting in the short history of the game, and it unsettled Brainard and the Red Stockings.

"Death to Flying Things" waved his bat around at Brainard as the Brooklyn crowd looked on in wonder at this surprise strategy. Ferguson, however, had a specific reason for employing the switch. He wanted to keep the ball away from George Wright at shortstop, who had been gobbling grounders and terrorizing the Atlantics on pop flies all afternoon. With Ferguson batting from the left side of the plate, he was less likely to hit the ball to George Wright.

The scheme worked perfectly. "Death to Flying Things" lined a whistling basehit into right field to score Start and tie the game at 7–7. In center field, Harry Wright began to wonder if maybe he should have called it a day back at the end of the ninth frame. The Brooklyn crowd was uproarious. The locals had tied the game once again, and now the mighty Red Stockings were on the ropes. George "The Charmer" Zettlein stepped up to take his licks, in a pitcher-versus-pitcher duel. Ferguson taunted Brainard off first as Zettlein waved his war club in a menacing fashion. Brainard ground the sphere into his hip, crossed his legs in his inimitable style, took a step forward, and then heaved the pea plateward. Zettlein smacked a hard grounder to the right of Charlie Gould at first base. "The Bushel Basket," in Buckneresque fashion, muffed the ball as the Atlantic cranks erupted. Ferguson steamed toward second. As "The Bushel Basket" retrieved the ball, he saw Ferguson, out of the corner of his eye, nearing the bag. Gould fired the ball in that direction, but wildly. The wayward sphere bounced into left field as Gould and his mates looked on in horror. Ferguson shot a glance behind him, saw Andy Leonard furiously chasing the ball, and joyously skipped around third and then homeward with the winning score. Atlantics 8, Red Stockings 7. The streak was over.

After the Atlantics made their final out, the Red Stocking nine stood frozen on the field, not believing that they were losers for the first time in almost two full seasons. Slowly, they walked off the dusky, paper-strewn Capitoline Grounds field as the remaining Atlantic cranks hooted and jeered them. "The yells of the crowd could be heard for blocks around and a majority of the people acted like escaped lunatics," the *New York Sun* reported of the postgame celebration.

It was the first loss in some ninety-five games for the Cincinnati Red Stockings. Ironically, the last loss also was at the hands of the Atlantics, way back on October 1, 1868. After the game, each Atlantic conqueror was voted a $364 bonus by the club's board of directors.[13]

Back at the hotel, Aaron Champion broke down and wept. He then composed the following telegram, and sent it back to the disbelieving hordes at the Gibson House:

NEW YORK, JUNE 14
    ATLANTICS 8, RED STOCKINGS 7. THE FINEST GAME EVER PLAYED. OUR BOYS DID NOBLY, BUT FORTUNE WAS AGAINST US. ELEVEN INNINGS PLAYED. THOUGH BEATEN, NOT DISGRACED.
A. B. CHAMPION
CINCINNATI BASE BALL CLUB[14]

One Cincinnati crank told the *New York Daily Tribune* that "the news of the defeat of the Red Stockings produced a great sensation here. During the progress of the game people stood by the hundreds in the street and around the newspaper offices, watching the result with an interest equal to that manifested during the [Civil War], when waiting for the news from the front. The excitement at the close of the ninth inning was intense."[15] Some buildings in the Queen City were draped in black after news of the crushing loss flashed across the wires.

While most of Gotham celebrated the great upset victory, some in the media were embarrassed that the key play in the Atlantic win appeared to have occurred when Brooklyn cranks interfered with Cal McVey as he attempted to track down Joe Start's fly ball. The *New York Herald*, in an article headlined "Defeated by a Brooklyn Crowd," lectured that "disinterested parties who were present assent positively that the visitors were obliged to play against the crowd, together with the opposing nine; that the crowd interfered with long hit balls, and that they received nothing like a fair show to win. To the initiated this is not remarkably strange as the same tactics have been practiced on previous occasions."[16]

The *New York Daily Tribune* waxed eloquent about the historic loss. "It is not in the power of the 'invincibles' to command success always, and the rich wreath which a year and a half's uninterrupted success had woven and won for the Red Stockings club was wrested from them ... and transferred to deck the conquering Atlantic club."[17]

The *Cincinnati Commercial* was philosophical about the loss: "It becomes the good people of our Queen City, to bear with philosophy the fact that the famous Red Stockings have at last been vanquished; no doubt the burden is grievous to be borne, but in the varied affairs of human life, the contemplative mind may find other things fully equal in importance to a first-class game of base ball."[18]

The *New York Clipper* had the most elegant account of the historic contest:

> If there is one feature of our national game of ball more than another which especially commends it to popularity, it is the fact of the glorious uncertainty attendant upon it. Hence, no matter how excellent in skill a nine may be, invariable success, season after season, is never at their command; and therefore no club can long monopolize that supremacy which all are ambitious of attaining, for the door is always left open for aspirants to baseball fame to enter the portals of the temple of the goddess and grasp the laurels in the face of the strongest opposition.[19]

21. The Face of Mortality

The day after the Red Stockings were sunk by the Atlantics, the now-mortal Cincinnatians went out and stomped the Morrisania Unions 14–0, behind the sparkling, four-hit shutout pitching of Asa Brainard, who had hurled twenty-nine innings of work over three consecutive days.

Four days after the disaster in Brooklyn, the Wright men faced another close call as they struggled to get by the Stars BBC at the same Capitoline Grounds. Thousands of Brooklynites converged at the ballyard, confident that the Stars could overturn the Cincinnati apple cart in the same manner that the Atlantics had. The *New York Daily Tribune* reported:

> Up the Brooklyn hills the over-taxed horses labored, and conductors elbowed through the crowd, while drivers and passengers vied in energetic remarks, directed more particularly against the weather, but occasionally favoring their more immediate neighbors. The scene at the Capitoline Grounds was a lively one. The sun shot down its intense rays upon the immense crowd without pausing to make any distinction of "age, sex, or color." The club-house windows looked bright with the gay colors and waving handkerchiefs of the lady spectators, while the fence extending around the grounds was lined with the heads of the non-paying witnesses. Every tree within sight was densely populated, while one individual of an enterprising turn of mind had brought a large wagon close to the fence, and erecting an extensive platform thereon, charged "ten cents a seat."[1]

This game featured Hall-of-Famer William Arthur "Candy" Cummings on the pitcher's point for the Stars. Cummings weighed in at a filament-thin 120 pounds, making him the lightest player in baseball history with the exception of Eddie Gaedel of 1951 St. Louis Browns fame. Cummings also was the first pitcher to make effective use of the curveball, a skill he acquired while amusing himself as a youngster by throwing clam shells and watching them sail through the air, turning to the left and the right as they flew. "All of a sudden it came to me that it would be a good joke on the boys if I could make a baseball curve the same way," the Candy man later chortled, and he experimented with his new pitch until he was able to master it in 1867 with the Excelsior BBC.

113

Cummings remembered the moment when he realized that his brilliant scheme was a success.

> In 1867, I, with the Excelsior Club, went to Boston, where we played the Lowells, the Tri-Mountains, and Harvard clubs. During these games I kept trying to make the ball curve. It was during the Harvard game that I became fully convinced that I had succeeded in doing what all these years I had been striving to do. The batters were missing a lot of balls; I began to watch the flight of the ball through the air, and distinctly saw it curve.
>
> A surge of joy flooded over me that I shall never forget. I felt like shouting out that I had made a ball curve; I wanted to tell everybody; it was too good to keep to myself.
>
> But I said not a word, and saw many a batter at that game throw down his stick in disgust. Every time I was successful I could scarcely keep from dancing from pure joy. The secret was mine.
>
> The baseball came to have a new meaning to me; it almost seemed to have life.[2]

Cummings's curve was not dancing altogether too successfully on this afternoon, but the Stars fought the Red Stockings feistily, and after six innings the match was knotted 11–11. The Brooklyn cranks taunted and jeered at the struggling Stockings who, after not having lost in almost two years, now were potentially facing their second defeat in a week, and in the same ballpark to boot.

Charlie Gould saved the day in the seventh inning, though, as he caught hold of one of Candy's curves and swatted it far over the heads of the Stars' flychasers for a three-run homer to break the tie and pace the Stockings to a five-run rally, and they held on for a hard-fought 16–11 triumph.

The road became more rocky for the Red Stockings now. They scored fewer and fewer runs, and the day-in, day-out fifty-run routs were becoming rarer and rarer. Teams played them with more confidence now, after the dethronement at the hands of the Atlantics. Every club now thought itself worthy of being a giant-killer.

On June 22 the Red Stockings traveled to Philadelphia for a tangle with the Athletics at the Athletic Base Ball Ground. Fifteen to twenty thousand rowdy Philly partisans packed the inside of the grounds, while outside thousands more sat just outside the park on temporary seats on carriages and brewery wagons and peered over the grounds' fences at the action inside. As the Red Stockings appeared at the park, the local cranks taunted them with the unbrotherly love-filled razz, "You're a-goin' to get beat! You're a-goin' to get beat!"

The contest was a matchup of two of the best pitchers in the game, iron man Brainard versus the Atlantics' Dick McBride, who would win forty-four games in 1875 for Philadelphia.

The Philadelphians bombed Brainard over the first two innings and, before they had a chance to catch a breath, Harry Wright's troupe found themselves on the short end of an 11–4 beating as the Philadelphia throng roared out its approval. Asa Brainard was sagging this afternoon, and the Cincy strikers knew that victory on this occasion would only come in the form of a high-scoring shootout. Cal McVey clubbed a towering homer off McBride in the third to pace the Stockings to a seven-run, game-tying rally. In the fourth, Cincinnati edged ahead, 16–15, for the first time in the tense contest.

By the eighth inning, Harry's hardballers had pushed out to a 25–21 lead, and it appeared that the combative Athletics had run out of gas just short of the finish line as they came to bat that inning. Brainard quickly notched the first two outs, but then the Atlantics began to stir. They pushed across a run to make it 25–22, and with two runners on, pitcher McBride stepped up to the plate. The Philly chucker was an unspectacular striker — his lifetime batting average was just .260 — and Brainard stared in at him confidently as McBride hollered out his pitch selection. Brainard checked the baserunners, went into his crazy, cross-legged pirouette, and chucked the pea homeward. Crack! McBride crushed the Brainard offering far over the heads of the Cincy fly chasers, and the Athletic hurler wheeled around the bags for a game-tying three-run homer. The Atlantic Base Ball Grounds shook as the ecstatic Philly fanatics bellowed forth their boisterous approval of the little hurler's big blow.

It was now 25–25 as the staggering Red Stockings batted in the top of the ninth. The late afternoon sun cast long shadows across the field and made it hard to pick up the ball as the pitcher unleashed it. George Wright squinted out at Dick McBride as he batted with one out. McBride's offering exploded out of the shadows at Wright, but he snapped his bat around and lashed a hard single back through the middle. The speedy Cincinnati shortstop then stole second base. Charlie Gould lofted a towering fly to center that was dropped by the Athletics' Count Sensenderfer. Wright scampered home and scored as Gould stormed into second. Fred Waterman then lined a Gould-scoring double, and the Stockings took a two-run lead into the bottom of the ninth.

Wes Fisler led off the Athletics' last licks with a screaming double, and the Athletic cranks roared anew, believing that their club was about to stage an Atlantic-like comeback. But Asa Brainard bore down. He induced Count Sensenderfer to ground out, then K'd George Shafer, and then got John Radcliff to pop up to George Wright to end the contest. As the falling orb settled into Wright's large hands, he squeezed it hard and then flashed one of his legendary toothy grins. The Red Stockings had survived with a nifty, come-from-behind 27–25 triumph.

The next day it was the same thing against the Keystone BBC. The Keystone held a 23–16 edge over the Red Stockings in the seventh inning, but roundtrippers by McVey, Leonard, and replacement Dean keyed a twenty-one-run comeback over the final three frames of the contest as the Carmine Hose clawed back triumphantly for the second game in a row, 37–26.

It got a little easier for the Red Stockings as they trekked southward through Baltimore and Washington, beating up on the Pastime, Maryland, Olympic, and National Base Ball Clubs. In the contest against the Nationals, Doug Allison wore a small glove — a "buckskin mitten" as the *Cincinnati Commercial* called it — to protect his sore hand, marking perhaps the first time in the history of the game that any player wore any sort of glove on his hand.

Returning home to Cincinnati afterward, the club found a somewhat smaller but still enthusiastic welcoming party at the railroad station than had greeted them a year earlier when they had returned from the East as nationally famous conquering heroes. The club rode carriages back to the Gibson House, where they had dinner that first evening home.

On July 1 there was a reception for the Red Stockings at Pike's Music Hall. The festivities included music and speeches lauding the ball club. One of the orators commented, "I feel satisfied that although they were beaten on one field once, that thing cannot be done again ... and having a Champion at their head, I think they will see to it that this thing does not happen again."

On July 2 the Red Stockings returned to the Union Grounds to joust with Albert Spalding and the Forest City BBC, with whom they had played on more than one occasion in 1869. A large crowd showed up to welcome back the red-legged nine to town, but quickly grew concerned when they noticed that George Wright was not in uniform for the contest. The Red Stockings' star shortstop had injured his knee while playing in Washington, and it still had not sufficiently healed for him to return to the infield. Instead, George was tapped to umpire the contest — a nod to his integrity and sense of fair play.

Once again the Red Stockings jumped all over Spalding and were up 10–3 early on. The Forest City crew crept back though, and found themselves behind 14–10, as they took their last raps in the ninth inning. Once again, the Red Stockings' grasp on victory was a little slippery. The Forest City nine roared back with three runs to cut Cincinnati's lead to one — helped in part by a rare muff by Harry Wright — before the tying run was cut down at home plate, and the Stockings escaped with an oh-so-close 14–13 squeaker.

Independence Day of 1870 dawned bright, hot, and sunny in Cincinnati. The downtown area was a loud and happy place all day as patriotic revelers lit firecrackers, shot off guns, and discharged cannons in celebration of the nation's ninety-fourth birthday.

At the Union Grounds, the Red Stockings readied for a rematch with

Forest City. Given the Fourth of July holiday and the celebratory atmosphere in the city, the Union Grounds were packed tight with cheery cranks, many of whom had brought small flags and firecrackers for the occasion. The *Commercial* described how, as game time approached, "all the seats were taken, yet the avenues leading to the grounds were densely thronged with people on the road 'to see the game.' At the time for the call of play, the crowd had been pressed inside the ropes and stretched along the embankment at the extreme boundaries of the grounds so that the police authorities were unable to keep them from interfering with some of the plays."[3]

George Wright was back in uniform for the July 4 tilt, and he and the Red Stockings cruised to a 24–7 holiday victory over Albert Spalding and his Forest City nine. After the contest, members of both clubs joined thousands of Cincinnati citizens downtown at the Fifth Street Market area for a fireworks show.

As Harry Wright and his men prepared for a road trip to Chicago, Aaron Champion and the directors of the Cincinnati Base Ball Club discussed the idea of expanding the Union Grounds. The bulging Independence Day crowd had convinced the directors that the time had come to expand the grandstand at the Union Grounds by lengthening it and adding a second tier to it. The additional seats would raise the capacity at the Union Grounds to approximately 8,000.

The Red Stockings, meanwhile, were meeting the Amateur BBC of Chicago. While this was not the mighty $10,000 White Stocking nine, nonetheless it was a Windy City ball club, and inasmuch as denizens of Cincinnati despised any Chicago squad — given the proclivity of that city's people and newspapers to label the Queen City "Porkopolis" — it was a delightful and satisfying afternoon for the Red Stockings and their fans as Harry Wright's lads laid it on against the Windy City amateurs, beating them 56–19. Both George and Harry Wright bashed prodigious circuit clouts in the blowout. Harry noted the impressive shots in his scorebook afterward, commenting that his was a "Home Run over fence," while brother George's four-bagger was the "longest hit on the game."[4] Ironically, while Aaron Champion and the club directors were back home discussing the expansion of the Union Grounds grandstand, the stands at the Chicago field collapsed, sending Windy City cranks flying all over the place. No serious injuries were reported, but many fans quickly decided that, in the future, the standing-room section would be a lot safer.

Two days after the match against the Amateur BBC, the Red Stockings journeyed up to Rockford to face the Forest City Club once again. In the first inning the Forest City crew jumped out to a quick 5–0 lead as George Wright and Cal McVey both muffed balls and Albert Spalding laced a two-run safety. The Red Stockings, however, rebounded with five tallies of their own to tie the score. The lead then volleyed back and forth for the remainder of the game, and at the end of nine innings the score stood at 16–16. By now dusk had settled in over the Forest City grounds, and the umpire waved off any further play due to the approaching darkness. There was nothing that Harry Wright could do about this one. There was no one to appeal to. It was simply too dark to continue to play. It also was the Red Stockings' second non-win of 1870. Cranks in the Queen City were shocked at the tie, particularly since the Red Stockings had trounced the Forest City nine on every other occasion in 1869 and 1970. But, just as a sea captain could pilot a ship hundreds of times across the ocean without incident, people remember only the one night that he smashed into an iceberg. In the same vein, the cranks in Cincinnati were now beginning to focus more on the two blemishes on the Red Stockings' record than on the squad's forty wins to that point in the 1870 campaign.

When the Red Stockings returned to Cincinnati after the Forest City tie, the bloom was off the rose. The *Commercial* and *Gazette* newspapers both began to criticize the team's play and attitude. When the Red Stockings barely beat the Harvard BBC, 20–17, at the Union Grounds, Harry Millar wrote that while the club had notched a "majority of the tallies, nobody would claim it as a victory."

The *Commercial* even went so far as to accuse the Red Stockings of throwing games. The paper suggested that Harry Wright's nine had intentionally let the July 2 Forest City game get close in order to build up interest in the July 4 rematch. The newspaper never offered any other concrete evidence to back up its charge, but nonetheless the accusation stuck.

The Red Stocking players themselves also took a bashing in the Cincinnati dailies now, particularly Doug Allison. The *Commercial* growled that Allison's "organ of self-conceit has been terribly enlarged this season.... The public expects work, and no fine airs, and no exhibitions of crooked temper and exaggerated self-importance." The *Gazette* blasted the Red Stocking backstop as well, harrumphing that "[his] lazy antics are utterly without excuse, and he does not gain any credit by indulging in them."[5]

With this suddenly negative backdrop, the Red Stockings faced the Philadelphia Athletics at the Union Grounds on July 27. Asa Brainard and Dick McBride matched goose eggs for three innings before the Athletics drew first blood in the fourth. In the fifth, the scrappy Philadelphians scored another quartet of tallies to make it 5–0. The Red Stockings finally got on the board by virtue of homers clouted by Charlie Gould and Andy Leonard, but in the top of the ninth the Stockings came up to bat for the final time, facing a 9–5 deficit. With two men on, Charlie Sweasy clocked a scorcher to left field that Athletic flychaser George Bechtel muffed. One run scored to make it 9–6 but, inexplicably, Asa Brainard, who had been on first base, stopped suddenly at second base when he easily could have motored to third and perhaps even scored himself. Sweasy, meanwhile, was running hard with his head down, and blasted into second base — and right into Brainard. It was a Keystone Kops baserunning situation, and Philadelphia second baseman Alfred Reach plunked a quick tag down on Sweasy for the second out. The next batter, Cal McVey, drove in the absentminded Brainard to make it 9–7, but George Wright shockingly was called out on strikes to end the inning. The Athletics added two meaningless runs in their at-bat in the bottom of the ninth. Thus it ended, Philadelphia 11, Cincinnati 7. It was the Red Stockings' first home loss since August 24, 1868. Cincinnati was Mudville for the first time in almost two years.

22. After the Fall

Three days after the loss to the Athletics, Harry Wright & Co. tangled with the New York Mutuals at the Union Grounds. By now, every club was gunning for the reeling Red Stockings. Back in the Big Apple, the Peck & Snyder Sporting Goods store at 126 Nassau Street — the self-proclaimed "Base Ball and Sportsman's Emporium" — displayed in its window the "Peck & Snyder Dead Red Ball" as a show of support for the Mutuals. Ironically, the Peck & Snyder boys, a year earlier, had printed one of the very first baseball cards in the pastime's history, albeit solely for promotional purposes. The club that Peck & Snyder had featured, so as to attract customers to its "Base Ball and Sportsman's Emporium": The 1869 Red Stockings, who they were now lampooning. Peck & Snyder also affixed to the front window telegrams updating the score of the Red Stockings–Mutuals game. Each inning a Peck & Snyder clerk would post a new telegram on the window, so that the cranks outside could follow the goings-on in Cincinnati.[1]

The Red Stockings, batting first at home, struck for a pair of runs in the first inning to take a quick 2–0 lead. By the fifth inning, the Scarlet Hose had cruised out to a 9–1 lead. At Peck & Snyder, Big Apple cranks soured at the bad news. The Mutuals, however, stormed back, scoring a half-dozen runs in the bottom of the fifth and single tallies in the sixth and seventh to tie the match at 9–9. The Red Stockings grabbed the lead back with a sole run in the top of the eighth, but in the bottom half of the frame, the New York nine plated a troika of runners to take a 12–9 lead into the ninth. At Peck & Snyder, hundreds of Mutuals fans roared and pounded on the panes of glass when the telegram showing the 12–9 lead was posted. Store proprietor Andrew Peck looked on nervously, fearful that one of the boisterous cranks was going to crash through the plate glass window and into his store.

In the top of the ninth, facing the prospect of their second home loss in less than a week, the red tide crashed onto the New York shore. George Wright singled in the game-tying score, and then Charlie Gould clouted a monstrous three-run roundtripper to give the sons of Cincinnati another come-from-behind triumph, 15–12. Groans were heard up and down Nassau Street after Andrew Peck himself posted the sad tale on the window pane. Mutual cranks tore up the woeful telegrams and trudged home, full of sorrow.

On August 2, at the monthly meeting of the Cincinnati Base Ball Club at Mozart Hall, Aaron Champion unexpectedly resigned as president of the club. Vice President Thomas G. Smith also quit his office, as did Secretary John P. Joyce. Champion stated that "business demands my attention more strictly than it is possible for me to give it and retain the office of president." Smith and Joyce similarly cited the claims of their private businesses as the reasons for resigning.[2]

The sudden, unannounced departure by the top three executives of the CBBC was shocking. There had been no advance warning that this was about to occur, and it threatened to leave the club rudderless at precisely the time that leadership was most necessary.

Newspaper reporters and cranks across the city wondered about the real reasons behind the sudden resignations. Had the disappointment from the recent losses, and the subsequent criticism of the club in the papers, driven Champion, Smith and Joyce to quit? Had rumors of growing discord on the club played a part in their decision? Champion himself later noted that by this point in the season the Red Stockings were beginning to segregate themselves into two separate camps, one of which consisted of the Wright brothers, McVey, and Gould, and the other that was made up of Sweasy, Waterman, Brainard, Allison, and Leonard. The latter group, in particular, consisted of players who were known to be insubordinate on occasion, and there was a feeling that perhaps the latter group was beginning to chafe under the authority of Harry Wright. Champion himself even noticed this. "There was a great jealousy existing between them," he later recalled. "The one side claimed that the Wrights were always assuming certain privileges exclusively for themselves, and the Wrights maintaining on the other hand that they only performed their duty." Of course, none of this tension and jealousy surfaced when the club was winning. It is likely that the pressure and criticism from the recent losses caused any such rift to expand.

Two weeks after the resignations of Champion, Smith, and Joyce, the Cincinnati Base Ball Club announced its new officers. A. P. C. Bonte was elected as the new president, Gibson House proprietor A. G. Corre was made the new vice president, and Will Noble — who reportedly had loaned the club his wife's $300 life savings before the start of the East Coast tour in 1869 — was named the club's new secretary.[3]

Champion, meanwhile, quickly announced that he was going to run for prosecuting attorney. Many saw this as perhaps the reason behind his sudden resignation. Champion, an astute lawyer and businessman, perhaps recognized that the recent losses suffered by the club, and the subsequent dissatisfaction of the cranks as seen in the lower number of rooters showing up at the Union Grounds for each game, did not bode well for the future of the Red Stockings as a profitable venture. Perhaps Champion saw these storm clouds on the hardball horizon and simply decided to bail out before things got any worse. He still had a sterling reputation in the community and could parlay it into the job of prosecuting attorney.

Back on the field, the Red Stockings still managed to play solid baseball. On August 8 the club got its revenge against the Troy Haymakers for their hippodroming antics of a year earlier with a 34–8 pounding at home. The new grandstand seats at the Union Grounds were ready for use, but only 2,500 cranks showed up for the contest, rendering the new seats ironically unnecessary. Even worse, George Wright seriously injured his knee in the victory. In the sixth inning, Wright attempted to steal second base. Just as he was reaching the bag, the Troy second baseman fell onto George's right leg. George fell into a heap on the ground and momentarily passed out from the pain. His Red Stocking mates rushed onto the field to assist him. Once George was revived, he struggled to get to his feet, but found that he could not put any weight on his right knee. Substitute Dean took George's place in the game as the star shortstop was carried off the field and taken to a nearby doctor for examination. He would be out of the Red Stocking lineup until October.

On August 26 the Red Stockings snatched victory from the jaws of defeat in a topsy-turvy tilt with the Riverside BBC in Portsmouth, Ohio. In a pattern of amazing symmetry, both clubs scored three runs in the first, five in the second, and five again in the third. The Riverside nine then proceeded to light up Asa Brainard for fourteen more runs over the next five innings to take a 27–23 lead into the top of the ninth inning.

The Riverside hurler, Fitzsimmons, quickly got McVey and Gould out, leaving Cincinnati just one out away from its third loss of the season. Fred Waterman then reached base when the Riverside shortstop muffed a pop fly. Doug Allison and Harry Wright then both singled, and all of a sudden there was life for the Red Stockings. Andy Leonard was up next. He barked out his pitch selection to Fitzsimmons, who now was sweating profusely in the late afternoon heat. Fitzsimmons checked the runners and fired homeward. Leonard swung and lifted a towering fly to left field. Cursing, Leonard slammed his bat down as the Riverside left fielder began to settle under the ball. At the last second, though, the Riverside flychaser lost sight of the ball in the late afternoon sun and gave a final lunge at it. He appeared to have speared the ball just before it crashed to the ground, and the umpire ruled Leonard out, which would have given the Riversides the win. But Harry Wright immediately raced over to the arbiter and appealed the call, claiming that the outfielder had dropped the ball. Wright and the umpire went out to left field to discuss the situation with the fielder. In an astonishing show of honesty on the diamond, the Riverside outfielder indeed admitted that he had in fact dropped the ball. Leonard was safe on board at first. Waterman and Allison scored, and now it was 27–25.

The next striker for Cincinnati was Asa Brainard. With two runners on, the mutton-chopped chucker cracked a sharp single to load the bags. Charlie Sweasy then strutted to the plate. Sweasy was the sixth Cincinnati striker to bat after the second out had been made in the inning. (Fans of the 1986 Boston Red Sox can probably understand the Riversides' predicament at this point.) Fitzsimmons stomped around on the pitcher's point, ready to throttle his left fielder for muffing Leonard's fly ball and gift-wrapping these extra opportunities for the Red Stockings to rally back. The big Riverside righty dragged a flannel sleeve across his sweaty brow and stormed back onto the iron point. He stared down Sweasy as the fireplug second sacker hollered out his pitch selection. The sun was setting behind the Riverside Base Ball Grounds now, and Sweasy was squinting out at the pitcher, trying to block out the glare that cut across the infield. Fitzsimmons peered at each Cincinnati runner on the three bags, wiped his moist hands across his sweat-soaked flannel shirt, and tugged at his jockey-style cap. He gripped the sphere in his fingers, lurched forward, and blazed a pitch in with an animalistic grunt. Sweasy, waving his small willow bat furiously, uncoiled and cracked a deep fly ball over the head of Rodwich, the center fielder. Fitzsimmons twisted around to watch the flight of the ball, screamed, and kicked a piece of sod in the air. Harry Wright scored easily, and Leonard was not far behind him. Brainard rumbled around the bags like a runaway train, and he scored also. As Rodwich finally caught up to the blast back near where extra Riverside cranks were standing at the edge of the outfield, Sweasy wheeled around the bases and stomped onto home plate with resounding glee. A grand slam! Sweasy was mobbed by his ecstatic mates as Fitzsimmons fired his cap to the ground, his neck muscles bulging out like ill-fitting cable wires. The Red Stockings had scored a half-dozen runs, all with two out, for an incredible come-from-behind 29–27 victory.

The Red Stockings were a festive band of baseballers as they boarded the steamship *Fleetwood* for the trip back up the Ohio River to the Queen City after the sensational comeback effort. Spirits flowed freely as the club celebrated the victory — perhaps a little too freely. At some point on the trip, Charlie Sweasy and a couple of other unnamed players began to argue and fight on board the ship. It got so unruly that the captain of the boat even threatened to run it ashore and throw the troublemaking ballplayers off.

When the story hit the Cincinnati newspapers, the CBBC and its new board of directors were not amused by the team's antics. Sweasy was expelled from the ball club for his "disgraceful conduct." By virtue of the expulsion, Sweasy also forfeited the remainder of his contract. Cincinnati Base Ball Club President A. P. C. Bonte also announced that the Red Stockings would be further purged of any and all "intemperate, insubordinate, and disorderly members."

The expulsion of Sweasy was met with mixed reviews. The *Cincinnati Times* lauded Bonte for his swift disciplinary move, stating: "This prompt action marks the newly-elected officers as eminently fitted for their duties.... Exit Sweasy. Who next?"[4] Others, however, saw the move as heavy-handed. While Sweasy clearly had been an embarrassment to the club on board the *Fleetwood*, nonetheless it appeared that jettisoning him was a little excessive. He was one of the best players on the club, his conduct notwithstanding, and the Red Stockings needed him at second base for the remainder of the 1870 campaign. It took Bonte only about twenty-four hours to realize this. Just one day after Sweasy was expelled from the club he was reinstated. A subdued and chastened Sweasy promised the CBBC board of directors and his teammates that his conduct would be nothing short of angelic for the rest of the season.

As the month of September appeared on the 1870 calendar, the Red Stockings had an opportunity to avenge their first loss of the season as they faced the Brooklyn Atlantics back home at the Union Grounds. The contest was heavily promoted as the rematch of the legendary June 14 affair at the Capitoline Grounds in Brooklyn, and Bonte fully expected that the enlarged grandstand at the Union Grounds would be packed to capacity for the epic contest. Thus, Bonte was disappointed when a crowd of only 6,000 cranks showed up for the game. Six thousand people still made quite a respectable showing, but Bonte wanted to bang the park out. He was hoping for 10,000 cranks if possible. Thus, having only 6,000 show up was a disappointment. Perhaps, Bonte thought, Aaron Champion had been right when he resigned from the club.

The 6,000 cranks in attendance did give Charlie Sweasy a healthy round of cheers when he appeared on the field with the rest of his teammates. The cranks had read the newspapers and knew of the rumors of his Fleetwood antics, but they basically let Sweasy know that all was forgiven. Sweasy responded to the cheers by repeatedly touching his cap in acknowledgment. Sweasy himself also had a fine contest that afternoon, cracking a home run and scoring three times himself as the Red Stockings atoned for their June 14 loss with a satisfying 14–3 victory in the rematch with the Atlantics.

After the contest, the recently resigned president of the Cincinnati Base Ball Club, Aaron Champion, hosted a ceremony on the field for the team, and he presented the Red Stockings with a silk banner from the lady members of the club. Champion remarked:

> I have the honor, on behalf of a number of ladies of our city, to present you this beautiful banner. These ladies desire in this token to express to you not only the pleasure they have felt in witnessing your play, but also wish to testify their approbation and delight that you have made the word 'Red Stocking' which is placed on this flag, famous throughout the country by your gentlemanly qualities, as well as by your abilities on the field. They hope that your

conduct will hereafter be as pure as the color of this flag on which the name is written, and that no stain shall ever be put upon it by your actions, but that it may remain white and unsullied as now.

As cheers rang out, Harry Wright responded in kind to Champion's generous remarks. "On behalf of this nine," Harry exclaimed, "I wish to say to these kind givers of this flag, that we sincerely thank them for this gift, and also thank them for the kind feelings (thoroughly appreciated by us) which induced it. We shall always carry this banner with us, and, though it may not on every occasion float over a victorious ball field, yet it shall ever wave over us as victors over all temptations."[5]

23. "Not a Porkopolian Has Heart Enough Left to Tell of the Defeat"

On September 7, the mighty Chicago White Stockings invaded the Queen City. Emotions were running high on the banks of the Ohio as the squad known as the "$10,000 Nine" stormed into town, led by such standouts as second baseman and team captain Jimmy Wood, hot cornerman "Long Levi" Meyerle, and pitcher Ed Pinkham. Hundreds of Chicago cranks traveled with the club to Cincinnati for the big match. The game was touted as the beginning of a rivalry on the level of the Red Sox and the Yankees today. "Either city is too proud to lose a game in which so much of the city's pride is involved," the *Commercial* remarked. "The game is emphatically Chicago vs. Cincinnati."[1]

Unfortunately for the Red Stockings, George Wright was still recuperating from his knee injury, and was not available for the game. As a result, Andy Leonard moved from left field to shortstop for the afternoon, and substitute Dean replaced Leonard in the outfield.

In the second inning the White Stockings, resplendent in their snow-white shirts, navy blue knickers, white hose, and navy blue caps with a white star on top, jumped all over Asa Brainard for three runs, keyed by a two-run double by Mart King and an RBI-single by pitcher Pinkham. The Red Stockings got a run back in the bottom of the fourth when Fred Waterman — who had gotten married just two days prior — scored on a passed ball. Ed Pinkham, however, was masterful on the pitcher's point. Some of the Red Stockings even stood behind the White Stocking catcher as they waited to bat, in hopes of being able to gain an edge on Pinkham. It was to no avail. By the bottom of the eighth, the Chicago lead was up to 8–1. The Scarlet Hose notched three tallies to cut it to 8–4, but the White Stockings added a pair of insurance runs in the top of the ninth. In the bottom of the final frame, the Red Stockings plated two additional runners, but when Charlie Sweasy popped out for the third out of the inning, the Chicago White Stockings were winners, 10–6.

The city of Cincinnati was appalled at the loss. It had been bad enough to lose to Brooklyn and Philadelphia, but this time it was the despised Chicago

White Stockings who had sunk the Red Stockings. Every other victory over the past two seasons was worthless, many Cincy cranks felt, if the Red Stockings could not beat the White Stockings, for now the Windy City instigators could resurrect the loathsome "Porkopolis" slur.

The Cincinnati Gazette fumed, "There is no excuse for the defeat. The Red Stockings were out-batted by the White Stockings and plainly beaten on the merits. But the absence of George Wright was a serious setback. The Red Stockings do not play with the same vim and energy with George out. And they were totally unable to hit Pinkham's pitching."[2]

The Gazette continued, "The umpire is a very nice sort of man but knew precious little of base ball. His decisions were given in a weak and faltering sort of voice and only after much hesitation. We hardly think Captain Harry Wright could have made a worse selection. A portion of the crowd disgraced itself by hissing constantly in the later portion of the game. Such demonstrations should be repressed in the future if Cincinnati is not to have the same reputation as that which gave the Haymaker grounds at Troy so unenviable a reputation."[3]

Back in Chicago, though, the gloating was at a fever pitch. When news of the victory was telegraphed back to the Windy City, according to the Chicago Tribune, the "cheers that rent the air made a considerable hole in the sky ... everybody determined upon a holiday. The banks were closed, the Courts and Board of Trade adjourned, and several people took a drink."[4]

The White Stockings returned to Chicago sporting scarves made up of small, red stockings. On the front seat of the White Stockings' carriage back in the Windy City sat a piglet wearing a pair of tiny, scarlet hosiery and carrying a placard that read: "PORKOPOLIS, SEPTEMBER 7, 1870."[5]

"Cincinnati was patriotic in the late ball-match," the Chicago Times chortled. "On the field were the red and white, and in the crowd, the blue."[6]

The Chicago Tribune boasted: "Our Cincinnati friends ... were routed, horse, foot, and dragoons, and not a Porkopolian has heart enough left to tell of the defeat ... it was necessary in order to teach the Cincinnatians a wholesome lesson. If they will profit by it, and learn that their place is on a back seat, Chicago ... in time may accord them the place of second best."[7]

24. The Dye in the Stockings Begins to Fade

The roasted Red Stockings hightailed it out of Cincinnati and regrouped with a 36–4 bashing of the Resolute BBC in Hamilton, Ohio, despite the unexplained absence of Asa Brainard. A day later, the Cincinnatians bombed the Dayton BBC 80–12 in a rout reminiscent of the games prior to their brief spurt of losses. Brainard did grace the Red Stockings with his presence on this occasion, although he was very late in showing up at the ball grounds. The *Dayton Herald* blasted Brainard, saying that the recalcitrant Red Stocking pitcher was "entirely too ceremonious, and manages to purposely absent himself, so as to show his importance. He is invariably late on the field, being the last man and the only one who causes vexatious delays."[1]

The Red Stockings continued to romp against more inferior clubs in late September. They humbled the Holt Jr. BBC on September 24, 32–7, at the Union Grounds as Charlie Sweasy led the way with a pair of roundtrippers. The Cincy second sacker was suddenly on quite a home run tear, having bashed eleven in his last nine games.

Harry Wright & Co. then invaded the Hoosier State and blasted the Indianapolis BBC 43–2 at the Indianapolis Fair Grounds. Journeying next to St. Louis, Asa Brainard handcuffed the Union BBC 28–1. Brainard allowed only one unearned run in the first, and then limited the Union nine to just four more hits on the rest of the afternoon — none after the fourth inning. At one point, the mutton-chopped master set down eleven Union strikers in a row between the fourth and seventh innings.

As autumn blazed across the Midwest in the first week of October in 1870, the sons of the Queen City teed it up against the Forest City BBC of Cleveland in another down-to-the-wire classic. Playing at the Union Grounds in front of only 2,500 bone-chilled cranks, the Forest City crew led 15–9 going into the bottom of the eighth frame when the Red legs staged another furious, late-inning comeback. Charlie Sweasy led off and reached on a two-base error. Cal McVey rapped a single to score Sweasy, and then McVey scooted to second on a passed ball. George Wright, finally playing again after a two-month hiatus forced by his injured knee, then grounded out, but Charlie

Gould swatted a triple, scoring McVey and making it 15–11. Gould then scampered home when Forest City catcher James "Deacon" White let the second passed ball of the inning get by him. After Fred Waterman popped out, Doug Allison doubled and scored on a Harry Wright safety. Now it was only 15–13. "Uncle Al" Pratt, hurling for the Forest Citys that afternoon, began to gulp on the pitcher's point, and likely reflected on the Riverside comeback staged by the Stockings six weeks earlier. Andy Leonard cracked a base hit to score Harry, making it 15–14. The Forest Citys were coughing it up. Leonard then daringly swiped second and third base on consecutive pitches. Asa Brainard was up next and, with the tying run in the form of Leonard leading off third, the Red Stocking hurler popped a lazy fly to Forest City third sacker Ezra Sutton who, in the spirit of his club's play that inning, promptly proceeded to drop the easy pop-up as Leonard steamed home with the tying score. Sutton got a chance to redeem himself on the next striker as Charlie Sweasy — who had started all of the trouble nine batters earlier — replicated Brainard's pop fly. This time, Ezra Sutton cradled the ball with such care that it looked like he was catching a baby being tossed from a burning building.

In the top of the ninth, with the score now 15–15, the Forest City lads went quietly, almost as if they already knew their fate. In the last half of the frame, the suddenly rejuvenated Queen City clouters strode to the plate with a renewed vigor. Cal McVey led off with a single off Uncle Al Pratt, who by now had to feel like a prisoner with his head on the chopping block, just waiting for the guillotine blade to fall. George Wright singled McVey to third. Wright then swiped second, showing one and all that his knee injury was fully healed. Gould popped to shortstop Parker for the first out. Fred Waterman stepped up next and rapped a double into the gap, scoring McVey and Wright and giving Cincinnati the lead and the win. Under 1870 rules, the Red Stockings still stayed at bat until three outs were made. Waterman took advantage of the situation by taking third and home on consecutive passed balls by the now-chastised Deacon White. The final score was Cincinnati 18, Forest City 15, in another heart-stopping conquest by the carmine-clad comeback crew.

October 13 proved to be another ill-starred afternoon for the Queen City nine. The day prior the club boarded a train on the Indianapolis, Cincinnati and Lafayette Railroad and chugged across the rails on a fourteen-hour trip to Chicago for a rematch with the gloating White Stockings at Dexter Park. The streets around the Windy City ballyard were clogged with hundreds of wagons, coaches, and carriages as some 15,000 cranks funneled into the park for the long-awaited rematch. Many of the Chicago cranks in attendance had copied the fashion of the White Stocking players and sported scarves knitted out of red stockings. The antagonizing piglet with the little scarlet hosiery also had bolted from the barnyard and showed up for the big game.

While the Red Stockings had staged several come-from-behind victories in the 1870 campaign, on this afternoon it would be the Pale Hose who would prevail in such a fashion. The Red Stockings mounted an early 5–1 lead over Chicago, but the White Stockings roared right back from the four-run deficit and the score stood at 8–8 entering the ninth inning.

In the top of the ninth, with the White Stockings at bat, Harry Wright, in a rare show of democracy, surveyed his mates as to who they thought should hurl the final frame. Brainard had started the contest, and Harry had relieved him on the pitcher's point in the eighth — but in this era it was allowable for a pitcher to be removed and then later returned to the point. "[The Red Stocking players] were unanimous in saying, 'Let Asa pitch,'" the *Commercial* reported.[2]

And so Brainard took to the pitcher's point in the top of the ninth, but the White Stockings whacked everything he offered up to them. They scored four quick runs before Harry Wright decided to end Brainard's misery and take over the pitching chores himself, something he probably regretted not doing in the first place at the start of the inning. So much for hardball democracy, Harry Wright must have thought to himself.

But even Harry himself could not stop the White Stocking onslaught in the top of the ninth. The Pale Hose plated eight men in the inning, and as the Red Stockings batted in the bottom of the frame, they trailed 16–8.

In the bottom of the ninth, though, the Stockings attempted to mount another furious comeback. Three straight safeties by George Wright, Charlie Gould, and Doug Allison led off the inning. Then Brainard also got on and Charlie Sweasy doubled, and when the score reached 16–13, the White Stocking cranks could feel those little red stocking scarves get a little bit tighter around their necks. But Ed Pinkham, the Chicago pitcher, reached deep into his reserve tank and stopped the Red Stocking rally cold at that point. Cal McVey made the game's final out on a grounder to third, and when it was all over and the White Stockings had won, 16–13, the Windy City cranks waved their red-stockinged scarves in the air, the scarlet-hosed piglet squealed with a porcine fervor, and the Chicago tabloids engaged in another generous round of Porkopolis-bashing.

The reeling Red Stockings silently trekked out of the Windy City and headed for a tilt with the Forest City BBC in Rockford on October 15. The Spalding gang already had tied the Stockings once in 1870, and now wanted to join the Atlantics, Athletics, and White Stockings as Goliath-slayers.

George Wright led off the Forest City game with a titanic clout deep into the pasture at the Rockford Fairgrounds to give the Stockings a 1–0 lead, and then brother Harry bashed a two-run job off Albert Spalding to make it 3–0 Cincy before many Rockford rooters had even entered the ballyard. Forest City got a pair back in their half of the inning, and then clubbed a troika of roundtrippers — by Gat Stires, Ross Barnes, and Albert Spalding himself — to snatch a 6–3 lead away from the battered Asa Brainard and his Red Stocking mates. It proved to be all of the offensive support that Spalding would need, as he handcuffed the Cincinnati strikers the rest of the way, setting down twelve in a row at one point, and the Forest City phenomenon notched his first victory against the Red Stockings, 12–5.

It was the second loss in a row for the suddenly beleaguered Wright men, the first time that that had happened since September 28–29, 1868, when they dropped back-to-back matches to the Athletics and the Keystones.[3]

The cranks back in Cincinnati were growing more and more disillusioned by the day, and they were particularly galled by the two losses to the hated White Stockings.

Eleven days later, the roof totally caved in as the Red Stockings lost again, 11–7, to the Atlantics in a match played in Philadelphia. It was the Brooklyn club's second triumph of the season against Cincinnati.

At first it appeared as if Harry's hardballers were going to pull another rabbit out of the hat in this match, as they had done so many other times in the summer of '70. The Red Stockings trailed the Atlantics 6–4 in the top of the ninth inning, and were down to their final out before Cal McVey and George Wright reached base on errors, and Charlie Gould drove them in with a clutch triple. "The Bushel Basket" then scored on a Fred Waterman safety to give Cincy a 7–6 lead.

The Red Stockings' success was short-lived, however, as the Queen City defense folded in the bottom of the ninth like a cheap accordion. Errors by Waterman, Sweasy, and Brainard — who personally muffed a pair of grounders and also heaved a wild pitch — opened the floodgates for the Atlantics, who appreciatively plated five tallies in their final at-bat for a gift-wrapped 11–7 victory. Charlie Sweasy and another unnamed teammate headed directly to a nearby Philadelphia saloon after the debacle to drown their sorrows, in violation of club regulations. CBBC President A. P. C. Bonte read Sweasy the riot act once again, but this time he did not expel the second sacker or even suspend him. It really did not matter at this point; any hopes of reclaiming the glory of 1869 had faded long ago.

The bloom was off the rose in Cincinnati. Like a suitor who stopped calling, the Queen City cranks stayed away in droves from the Union Grounds as the 1870 campaign came to a conclusion in early November. In the final home game of the season, only a couple of thousand cranks showed up to watch the Red Stockings trounce the New York Mutuals 23–8 and all throughout the contest the sound of bat meeting ball echoed loudly off the sparsely filled Union Grounds grandstand. After the contest, each Cincinnati player received a new silk hat as a memento of the season, but it was a hollow gift indeed.

Cincinnati Base Ball Club Secretary Will Noble decided to make one last effort to bring in some final gate receipts for the 1870 season, and he wired the Chicago White Stockings concerning another two-game series between the clubs:

> WE CHALLANGE YOU TO A SERIES OF GAMES, PRACTICE OR OTHERWISE, THE FIRST TO BE PLAYED HERE ON MONDAY, NOVEMBER 7, THE SECOND TO BE PLAYED IN CHICAGO ON WEDNESDAY, NOVEMBER 9.

The White Stockings counteroffered:

> WILL YOU PLAY FIRST GAME HERE ON MONDAY, WE TO TAKE ALL RECEIPTS. IF WE PLAY YOU RETURN GAME IN CINCINNATI, WEDNESDAY, YOU TAKE ALL RECEIPTS; THE GAMES TO BE PRACTICE, AND NOT AFFECT THE CHAMPIONSHIP.[4]

Will Noble rejected the White Stocking counteroffer out of hand. The Cincinnati nine trekked to Cleveland for their final game on November 5 and dumped the Forest Citys, 27–16. It marked the end of what was still an altogether successful season for the club victorywise, but the cranks in Cincinnati had come to expect perfection, which is what the club had given them in 1869. Anything less was unacceptable. Defeat had meant dishonor to the Queen City cranks. The Red dye was fading from the stockings, and the Hose had begun to run.

25. The Death of a Base Ball Club

Despite what the Cincinnati cranks would have had one believe, the 1870 Red Stockings were hardly forerunners of the 1899 Cleveland Spiders or even the '62 Mets. The club finished the season with sixty-eight wins, six losses, and one tie — a blistering winning percentage of .919. They outscored the opposition 2,732 points to 648 for an average margin of victory of 36–9 — good enough to be labeled a dynasty in football, let alone baseball.[1]

Charlie Sweasy was the club's home run king in 1870, although he clubbed only eighteen roundtrippers — a dozen less than his season total in 1869. George Wright's circuit-clout production fell from forty-nine in 1869 to fifteen in 1870. Leonard and McVey each swatted eleven homers, Gould ten, Harry Wright seven, Fred Waterman four, Asa Brainard three, and Doug Allison one. George Wright's batting average "fell" from .633 in 1869 to .536 in 1870. It's tough to imagine that old George lost much sleep fretting about falling below the Mendoza line.

In actuality, the Cincinnati Base Ball Club members and cranks had been severely spoiled by the team's success in 1869. Thus, when defeat eventually appeared in 1870, it was unbearable to the local crankdom. The Red Stockings were no longer the pride of the Queen City; they were just another ball club in another Midwest town.

Despite the team's fantastic success on the field, it was not a box office smash. With each loss in 1870, crank interest waned, and the gate severely declined from what the club had hoped for. As in 1869, the 1870 profit margin was thinner than boarding house soup.

The *New York Sun* reflected on the popular demise of the Red Stockings in the Queen City:

> Disappointment and chagrin marked the visage of every man, woman and child in Cincinnati who had the interest of the team at heart, and gloom like a pall spread over the town. The people of Redland could not realize that their great team had been beaten after going nearly two years without losing a game. Then, to add insult to injury, along came Chicago's 'White Elephant' … and gave the Reds another beating. Whether or not the feeling of weariness that was manifested throughout Redland had seized the players has never been stated, but it is a fact that they lost games quite frequently after their

first defeat, and as the Reds had not been a great financial success, the enthusiasm in Redland petered out as the season waned.²

Some newspaper reporters also believed that Harry Wright had lost a modicum of control over his charges. Toward the end of the 1870 season, after the Red Stockings had lost a couple of games, the *New York Clipper* reported that the Cincinnati nine was going to be thoroughly reorganized for 1871, in order to eliminate the "growlers and shrinkers" on the roster.³ This clearly was an allusion to the mercurial Brainard, and also likely to Sweasy and Allison, and perhaps Waterman as well.

Additionally, it appeared as though too much consumption of alcohol may have affected some of the Red Stockings players, particularly Brainard, who was an occasional no-show at contests after a long night on the town, and Sweasy, who raised a ruckus on the steamboat and entered a saloon in Philadelphia in full uniform after the second loss to the Atlantics. The *Commercial* announced that, with respect to signing up players for the 1871 campaign, "No player will be accepted next year who will not contract to abstain from intoxicating beverages at all times ... unless ... prescribed by a physician in good standing."⁴ In reality, though, no matter how much of a taskmaster Harry Wright was, he could not keep tabs on the likes of a Brainard or Sweasy twenty-four hours a day, and some style of bacchanalia was bound to occur from time to time.

At the same time, other clubs openly began to approach the Red Stocking players about leaving Cincinnati. George Wright was reportedly offered $3,000 to join a new club forming in Washington for the 1871 season. Asa Brainard, Charlie Sweasy, and Fred Waterman also received feelers from the new Washington club.

In the meantime, Cincinnati Base Ball Club President A. P. C. Bonte informed Harry Wright that the money just was not there to keep his nine intact. CBBC executives estimated that it would take some $16,000–$17,000 to cover the costs of player salaries, Union Grounds upkeep, and costs for uniforms, equipment, and advertising for the 1871 season, and the club would have to net about $500 per game over approximately 34 games in order to keep the club in the black — a financial feat that simply was not possible. The Red Stockings, for all of their on-field success, still were barely able to keep their financial head above water. Over the course of the 1869 and 1870 seasons, it was a constant struggle to meet the payroll and pay all of the bills each month. Things got so bleak that lumber had to be sold from the Union Grounds in order to pay off various creditors.

Finally, on November 21, 1870, Bonte released the following circular:

DEAR SIR: — According to custom, the Executive Board reports to the members of the CINCINNATI BASE BALL CLUB its determination in reference to the baseball season of 1871. We have had communication with many of the leading baseball players throughout the country, as well as with the various members of our former nine.

Upon the information thus obtained, we have arrived at the conclusion that to employ a nine for the coming season, at the enormous salaries now demanded by professional players, would plunge our club deeply into debt at the end of the year.

The experience of the past two years has taught us that a nine whose aggregate salaries exceed six or eight thousand dollars can not, even with the strictest economy, be self-sustaining.

If we should employ a nine at the high salaries now asked, the maximum sum above stated would be nearly doubled. The large liabilities thus incurred would result in bankruptcy or compel a heavy levy upon our members to make up a deficiency. We are also satisfied that payment of large salaries causes jealousy, and leads to extravagance and dissipation on the part of the players, which is injurious to them, and is also destructive of that subordination and good feeling necessary to the success of a nine.

Our members have year after year contributed liberally for the liquidation of the expenses incurred in the employment of players. We do not feel that we would be justified in calling upon them again; and, therefore, for the reasons herein stated, have resolved to hire no players for the coming season. We believe that there will be a development of the amateur talent of our club, such as has not been displayed since we employed professionals, and that we will still enjoy the pleasure of witnessing many exciting contests on our grounds. We take this opportunity of stating that our club and grounds are entirely free from debt; and, deeming it our first duty to see that they remain so, we pursue the course indicated in this circular.

For the Executive Board,

A.P.C. BONTE, President.

WILL P. NOBLE, Secretary.

Some believed that the Bonte blustering was merely a tactic designed to get the Red Stocking players to agree to lower salaries for the 1871 season.[5] It is unclear whether this analysis is necessarily the correct one in this case. The club did indeed discuss new contracts with the various Red Stocking players, albeit at amounts far less than the players desired. And, the CBBC even went so far as to enter into preliminary negotiations with Albert Spalding and other stars about joining the Red Stockings for the 1871 season. Again, though, the discussions never got very far. The CBBC Executive Board simply could not justify spending such exorbitant amounts of money on player salaries, particularly given the fact that fan interest had plummeted the way it did at the end of the 1870 season. There was simply too much of a financial risk to raise salaries for 1871. The club could not pay players without money coming in from ticket sales. Thus, it clearly could be argued that perhaps Bonte's circular was merely a ruse to get the Red Stocking players to play for less money. On the other hand, it is entirely reasonable to conclude that Bonte and the other members of the CBBC Executive Board made their decision strictly by the numbers — the numbers in the club's ledger books. It may not have been a ruse at all, but rather a stone-cold business decision and nothing more.

At the same time in Boston, a businessman named Isaac W. Adams was engaged in the establishment of a professional baseball nine for the Hub. Adams closely observed the situation in Cincinnati and wired George Wright about the prospect of his joining the newly formed Boston club. Wright wired back and told Adams of his interest in the new club. George apparently had made up his mind that he would not be returning to Cincinnati under any circumstances in 1871. He reportedly told associates that he would not play for the Red Stockings even for $2,500 a season, and he also became upset when Bonte criticized him and his brother Harry in a newspaper interview. Bonte told the *Cincinnati Times* that the salary demands of the Wright brothers were outrageous. He then went on to add, "They are good players beyond a doubt, but the papers have been so loud and extravagant in their praise that, to be frank, their heads are turned, and they seem to consider that we can not get along without them."[6] When the Wrights read Bonte's words in the *Times*, it solidified their decision not to return to the Queen City.

In late November of 1870, Harry Wright traveled east and met with Isaac W. Adams and the other organizers of the new Boston club at the Parker House in the city. On November 30, Harry announced to the sporting press that he had accepted Adams' offer to become the new manager, captain, and secretary of the Boston club at a salary of $2,500 a year. Less than two months later, it was announced that George Wright would be joining his brother in Beantown.

Adams consulted with the Wrights about signing other former Red Stocking players, and before long Charlie Gould and Cal McVey were on their way east to join George and Harry on the new Boston club. It is not at all surprising that Harry did not elect to pursue Asa Brainard, Charlie Sweasy, Doug Allison, or Fred Waterman for the new team he was piloting; he was quite content to let the "growlers and shrinkers" of the Red Stockings seek employment elsewhere.

It was a swift and mortal blow to early professional baseball in Cincinnati. Not only was almost half of the former Queen City nine now under contract in Boston, but Harry and George Wright had even gone so far as to take the Red Stockings name and Margaret Truman's custom-made hosiery with them. The loss of the Wright brothers sounded the death knell for the legendary Cincinnati Red Stockings.

Few tears were shed over the demise of the Cincinnati club. Even Bonte coldly stated, "You can wave the Star Spangled Banner, and talk about the glory of the Red Stockings, and the nine that meets with no defeat, but you must put your hands in your pockets and pay the bills. You can't run the club on glory."

The *New York Times* summed up the feeling of many when it opined how

> certain evils have followed in the train of professional ball-playing, which, if not checked in their progress, will ultimately so damage the reputation of the fraternity as to materially interfere with the future welfare of the game.... The fact is, the fraternity of Cincinnati and especially the class who have had to put their hands deep in their pockets in order to insure the success of the professional experiment, have begun to realize the fact that the credit and renown attached to the success of the professional nine of the Club does not inure to the credit of the Club as a Western organization, from the fact that the players who have won the laurels are experts who belong to the East. Not fancying this style of things any longer, they now propose to organize a nine on the footing of employing only amateur talent and home players at that. In this the Club do wisely, for despite the victories obtained by the three professional nines of Cincinnati, Chicago, and Cleveland, this season, the career of the Rockford nine, in reality, is the most credible of all the Western organizations, inasmuch as their success has been obtained at the hands of bona fide Western players. This example the Cincinnati Club propose to follow in 1871, in which year they will endeavor to bear off the palm of supremacy in the amateur arena, as they did in 1869 in the professional circle.[7]

Harry Ellard penned a most eloquent eulogy to the historic Red Stockings, the first all-professional ball club:

> And so it was that the great baseball club which has made our Cincinnati the cradle of our professional national game, passed out of existence, to live only in the memories of those enthusiastic lovers of the sport who can, during their hours of reminiscences, recall the time when they were young and cheered for the old Red Stockings in the days of "Auld Lang Syne."[8]

26. A New City, a New League

The NABBP languished as the Red Stockings disbanded and auctioned off all of their equipment, balls, bats, uniforms, streamers, medals, and trophies. The association was rife with problems that it had neither the heart nor stomach to eliminate. Players continued to jump from club to club in blatant disregard of contractual obligations; teams failed to show up for matches, particularly if it was late in the season and the gate was going to be small; silk-hatted umpires were subjected to an endless torrent of verbal and physical abuse by players and cranks; and there was still an inordinate amount of open gambling in the stands. The *Boston Herald* lamented how it was "the business feature of the game that was bringing it into disrepute."[1]

In 1871 the NABBP, toothless and decrepit, ceased operations. According to Albert Spalding; "The death of the National Association of Base Ball Players … was expected, natural and painless…. The organization had outlived its usefulness; it had fallen into evil ways; it had been in very bad company; and so, when the hour of its dissolution came, no sorrowing friends were there to speak a tearful farewell."[2]

In its stead emerged the National Association of Professional Base Ball Players, founded on St. Patrick's Day, 1871, in Collier's Saloon at the corner of Broadway and Thirteenth Street in New York City. There were ten original member clubs, including the Philadelphia Athletics, Forest Citys of Rockford, Forest Citys of Cleveland, Chicago White Stockings, Troy Unions, New York Mutuals, Washington Olympics, Washington Nationals, Fort Wayne Kekiongas, and the Wright brothers-led Boston Red Stockings. The Brooklyn Eckfords, dubious about the prospects that the NAPBBP would succeed, refused to pay the $10 admission fee to join the league when it was established, but hitched on in August of 1871 when the Kekionga nine disbanded.[3]

The Philadelphia Athletics were the first NAPBBP champions in 1871, sporting a 22–7 record. Harry Wright, however, was dismayed to learn that the Athletics displayed their championship pennant in a local saloon in Philadelphia. Wright urged the Athletics to display their flag in their own clubhouse, because "to elevate the National Game we must earn the respect of all; and now the Athletics are Champions—first legal and recognized Champion of the United States—they will be looked up to as the exponents of what is right and wrong in base ball, and will have it in their power, in a great measure, to make the game a success — financially and otherwise."

The Wright-led Red Stockings, now of Boston, finished third in 1871 despite being the preseason favorites of most of the era's baseball prognosticators. The most star-crossed club of all the NAPBBP was the White Stockings. On October 8, 1871, the Great Chicago Fire ravaged the city's central business district and left 300 dead and 90,000 homeless. The White Stockings' base ball grounds were destroyed in the tragic blaze, along with all of the club's uniforms and equipment. The White Stockings were forced to play the remainder of the 1871 season on the road, using uniforms, bats, and balls borrowed from other clubs. The White Stockings then bowed out of the NABBP for two years, as they and the rest of Chicago regrouped and rebuilt the city from the ashes.[4]

The NAPBBP lasted for five years, through 1875, and its legacy was a sorry history indeed.

All of the problems that had plagued the NABBP continued to fester in the NAPBBP and once again the new league was incapable of policing all of its hardball malefactors. Betting on contests continued to occur on a regular basis, as gamblers practically outnumbered pure spectators at some games. As a result, a large amount of hippodroming continued in the game. Players occasionally showed up for games drunk, and the stands as well were often filled with loud, inebriated, profanity-spewing louts, which kept women, children, and entire families away from the ballparks. In addition to everything else, many of the NAPBBP clubs had severe financial problems. Payrolls frequently were not met, and players continued to revolve from club to club on an alarmingly common basis. The league was a mess.[5]

During the fall of 1875, William A. Hulbert, president of the Chicago White Stockings, prepared plans for a new league to replace the ailing NAPBBP. Hulbert garnered support for his new league from clubs in Cincinnati, St. Louis, and Louisville, and added Harry Wright as a backer as well. In February 1876, at a meeting in New York City, Hulbert presented his proposal for a new league to additional representatives from Boston, Hartford, New York, and Philadelphia, and they agreed to join Cincinnati, St. Louis, Louisville, and Chicago in Hulbert's new league. In the spring of 1876, the new National League of Professional Baseball Clubs began play.[6]

27. "A Remarkable Band of Ball Players"

Albert Spalding, in a 1907 letter, summed up the legendary Red Stockings in the following manner:

> The old Cincinnati 'Red Stockings' of 1869 and '70 have immortalized Cincinnati in a baseball sense, for the wonderful success of that first professional team made its lasting impression on professional baseball. While it naturally stood out prominently as the best baseball club of the period, and while no doubt this prominence was in a great measure due to the fact that it was the only full-fledged professional team in existence at that time, yet no one can gainsay but that the Cincinnati "Red Stockings" of 1869 were a remarkable band of ball players.[1]

After the 1870 season and the death of the legendary Cincinnati Red Stocking club, the immortal nine scattered across America to other professional teams and other grassy fields. The Red Stockings' legacy to the National Pastime is as integral to the game as are the red stitches that keep a baseball from unraveling.

Asa Brainard

Asa Brainard joined the Washington Olympics in the NAPBBP in 1871, where he went 13–15 and batted only .200. After an even worse season in 1872 with the Middleton Mansfields (0–3, .161 batting average), Brainard jumped back to Washington, and then finished his career with the Lord Baltimores in 1874 and 1875. Brainard never had a winning season after leaving Cincinnati, although Harry Wright did write a friend that "the Bostons ... cannot hit the Count ... his old confidence must have returned."[2]

The mercurial Red Stocking ace later deserted his wife Mary, leaving her impoverished and alone to raise their infant son, Truman Brainard. In 1882, while running an archery range at Port Richmond, Staten Island, New York, Brainard was struck in the back of the hand by an arrow and seriously injured.[3]

Later that same year, Brainard began to correspond with his old manager, Harry Wright. Brainard had become bored and depressed after the arrow accident, but relished the memories of his old Red Stocking days, as rekindled by a Harry Wright missive. Brainard wrote back to Wright: "Your letter brings sweet remembrances of old days, we worked together so successfully.... [I am] waiting anxiously for something to turn up. I am living with my Mother on Staten Island.... What has become of McVey, Allison, Leonard, and others? I never hear of them, I thought they were on the retired list."[4]

Later, Wright wrote back to Brainard and updated him as to the whereabouts of his former mates, for which Asa was grateful: "I was pleased to hear how the Old Boys were situated and shall endeavor to let them hear from me."[5]

Brainard also pleaded with Wright to assist him in landing a job in the National League as an umpire: "I know you have got influence enough to make me one, and I think it but fair that you should. I am in want of something to do, and think it little enough for the base ball community to give to one who has done so much to elevate the game.... I have had hard luck since leaving the Ball field.... Harry, I am very anxious to get away from here and the City, as I think opportunities are better offered by traveling around the country. Make an effort in my behalf and you will get your reward."[6]

Asa Brainard never became an umpire. He later moved to Denver and operated a pool hall in that city, and he died there of pneumonia on December 29, 1888, at age 47, the first of the legendary Red Stockings to pass on.[7]

Doug Allison

Doug Allison also jumped to the Washington Olympics in 1871, where he hit .333, and then spent the next four seasons bouncing from the Brooklyn Eckfords to the Troy Haymakers to the New York Mutuals to the Elizabeth Resolutes to the Mutuals again and then to the Hartfords. Allison stayed in Hartford and hitched on with that city's National League franchise in 1876. He then bolted to Providence in 1878 and finished his career with Baltimore in 1883. The gritty Red Stocking backstop later worked as a day laborer in Washington, and he died there at age 70 on December 19, 1916.

Charlie Gould

The only native Cincinnatian on the Red Stockings, "the Bushel Basket" joined the Wright brothers and Cal McVey on the Boston Red Stockings in 1871. He was the starting first baseman on the 1872 Hub pennant winners.

While in Boston, Gould and the Wrights opened a sporting goods store on Boylston Street, and Gould even sat out the 1873 season in order to fully devote his time to the sporting goods business.

In 1874, though, Gould was back in the game, this time with the Lord Baltimores. A year later he was named player-manager of the New Havens, but his ragged crew staggered through an abysmal 7–40 campaign. In 1876, The Bushel Basket returned to the city of his glory days as he piloted Cincinnati's inaugural National League entry, albeit to an even worse record (9–56) than his horrendous New Haven nine had notched.

Gould ended his playing career in Cincinnati in 1877, but he stayed on with the club for three years as the team's assistant secretary and head groundskeeper. Gould also worked for the police department and the sheriff's office in Cincinnati after his playing days were over. He later moved to New York to live with one of his sons.

On April 10, 1917, Gould died at the home of his son, Charles Fisk Gould, in Flushing, New York. After his death, Gould's body was returned to Cincinnati and was buried in the Gould family plot at the Spring Grove Cemetery. A marker, however, never was placed on the grave. In 1951, Cincinnati Reds president Warren Giles launched a campaign to erect a monument at the site of Gould's final resting place, and an impressive memorial was placed at the grave of the Bushel Basket.[8]

Charlie Sweasy

Sweasy joined Asa Brainard and Doug Allison on the 1871 Washington Olympics, and he too lasted just a single season in the nation's capital. He jumped to the Cleveland Forest Citys in 1872, and then signed on with the Boston Red Stockings in 1873, where he played but a single game for the repeat pennant winners. There appeared to have been another conflict of some sort between Sweasy and Harry Wright during his short stay in Boston, for shortly before the start of the 1874 season Wright released Sweasy from his Boston contract and allowed him to hitch on with the Brooklyn Atlantics. Wright went so far as to advise the Brooklyn management concerning Sweasy; "When you draw up his contract you cannot make it too strict. He will do well if kept well in hand and looked after sharply. 'New brooms sweep clean.' The middle and latter part of the season they get shaky and loose…. I have talked to Sweasy very plainly, and should he fail this season, it would be his last."[9]

Sweasy wound up playing only ten games for the Atlantics before moving on to the Lord Baltimores in 1874. There he developed rheumatism, which forced the end of his playing career. The next year he was named manager of the St. Louis Reds. His nine was almost, but not quite, as bad as Charlie Gould's

New Havens, as the sons of Charlie Sweasy tottered to a 4–14 mark, finishing 36½ games behind the perennial Red Stocking champions. The '75 St. Louis Reds had a team batting average of an anemic .181.

In 1876, Sweasy played under former mate Gould back in Cincinnati, finishing his ball career in Providence in 1878. He then returned to his native Newark, where he worked as an oyster peddler for many years before he died on March 30, 1908, at age 60.

Fred Waterman

Waterman was another of the five ex–Red Stockings to sign with the Washington Olympics in 1871, and he was the only one of the five to sport a Washington uniform for longer than a single season. Waterman manned the hot corner for the Olympics for two campaigns, batting .305 in 1871 and .400 in 1872. In 1873 he moved across town to play for the Washington Nationals, ending his playing days in Chicago with the White Stockings in 1875.

Fred Waterman spent the rest of his days performing odd jobs around Cincinnati. He died there a pauper on December 16, 1899, at age 54.

Andy Leonard

Leonard joined Asa Brainard, Doug Allison, Charlie Sweasy, and Fred Waterman on the '71 Washington Olympic nine. The Hibernian hardballer latched on with his four other ex-Cincinnatians in Boston in 1872, at a salary of $1,800 a season, and played on all six of the Hub's champion Red Stocking squads between 1872 and 1878. Leonard returned to Cincinnati in 1880, but retired midway through the season due to failing eyesight.

Leonard worked for the Newark Water Department after his playing career ended. He then moved to Boston and toiled for George Wright at the Wright & Ditson Sporting Goods Company until his death from a gastric ulcer on August 22, 1903, at age 57, in Roxbury, Massachusetts. Cap Anson remembered Andy Leonard as "a splendid judge of high balls, a sure catch ... a swift and accurate long-distance thrower ... a good batsman and a splendid baserunner."[10]

Cal McVey

McVey switched to catcher after he left Cincinnati, and was the star backstop for the Boston Red Stockings in 1871 and 1872. McVey walloped a .419 batting average in '71 and led the NAPBBP in at-bats.

In 1873, at the tender age of 22, he was named manager of the Lord Baltimores, who went a respectable 23–14 under boy wonder McVey, good enough for a third-place showing that season. McVey jumped back to Boston in 1874, where he patrolled right field for the NAPBBP champs, batted .382, and led the league in at-bats and runs scored. He also was a member of a group of players who traveled to Great Britain to introduce the game of baseball to the English and the Irish.

McVey moved to first base for Boston in 1875 and clubbed opposition pitching to the tune of a .352 batting average. In 1876 McVey changed Stockings, going from Red to White, and played on his fourth pennant winner in five seasons. The versatile Iowan even pitched in eleven games for the White Stockings in 1876, going 5–1 with a nifty 1.52 earned run average and two saves.

In 1878 McVey managed the Cincinnati National League nine to a 37–23 second-place showing. The '78 Cincinnatians were particularly inept defensively, committing an amazing 269 errors in sixty games played. The only club more bumbling in the field than that club was the 1879 Cincinnatians, also managed by McVey, who butchered a staggering total of 454 balls, and probably were forbidden from using the cutlery in any of the hotel dining rooms they visited that season.

Cal McVey moved to San Francisco in 1880 and played with the Bay City Athletics and the San Francisco Pioneers before retiring in 1885. After his playing days ended, McVey settled in the Bay Area.

In 1906, McVey's home was destroyed in the great San Francisco earthquake. His wife also was severely injured in the massive calamity. McVey himself was forced to dwell in a shack on public property for a period of time with other displaced survivors of the great earthquake. In a letter to *The Sporting Life*, McVey wrote about his tribulation:

> I saved my wife, who is an invalid, and my father, who is 82 years of age, but nothing else in the world. You cannot appreciate the situation here. There are now 100,000 people homeless and destitute, and not one-tenth have a chance for work. I am trying hard to get away from here. Everything sent here in the shape of food and clothing has been ransacked and plundered by the so-called relief committees. It's simply awful. We are in a little 10' by 12' shack, sleeping on the ground. It rains almost every day, our imitation house leaks like a sieve, and it takes a lot of nerve to battle for life.[11]

Hard times would revisit McVey seven years later in Nevada when he fell thirty feet down a mine shaft and struck his abdomen against a scantling. The injury severely crippled McVey and left him unable to work full-time. As a result, McVey soon fell on hard financial times.

In 1914, McVey's former teammate Doug Allison sent a heartfelt petition to the National League, asking it to render financial and medical assistance to McVey, given the fact that the mine accident had left him in such dire straits. Allison's letter read:

> I have just received a sad letter from Cal McVey telling me he is down and out through a mine accident. His playing on the old Cincinnati "Red Stockings" helped to put base ball on the map of today, and [he] was one of the greatest players of his day. Cannot the National League put him on the retired list say at $40 or $50 per month[?] He also tells me if he could put himself under a good doctor he might be able to do some work.... Please do what you can on his behalf. By doing so you will greatly oblige one of his many friends.... I remain yours respectfully, Doug Allison, Washington, D.C., Catcher of the Cincinnati Reds.[12]

Cal McVey lived for another dozen years, and recuperated just enough to work at one point late in his life as a night watchman for a San Francisco lumber company. He died in San Francisco on August 20, 1926, at age 75.

In 1968, Cal McVey posthumously was inducted into the Iowa Sports Hall of Fame for his role as a member of the first all-professional baseball club in 1869.[13]

George Wright

Cincinnati's greatest star in 1869 and 1870, George Wright joined his brother Harry, along with Charlie Gould and Cal McVey, in forming the first NAPBBP dynasty, the Boston Red Stockings. The historic Hub hardballers won four straight pennants between 1872 and 1875, with King George leading the way at shortstop. In his first five seasons in Boston, Wright notched batting averages of .409, .336, .378, .345, and .337. The Boston club also won two of the first three National League flags, in 1877 and 1878, with Wright alternating between shortstop and second base. While in Boston George opened a sporting goods store, later taking on a partner and becoming known as the Wright & Ditson Company. Andy Leonard would work for Wright at the Boston sporting goods store. Albert Spalding, who was the stopper of the sensational Stockings of the '70s, and Alfred Reach also formed sporting goods companies, and the firms of Wright, Spalding, and Reach eventually merged, which proved to be extremely lucrative for George Wright.

In 1879, Wright became the manager of the Providence National League entry, and he led the Rhode Islanders to a 59–25 pennant-winning season. Wright also started at shortstop in that championship campaign, and his club led the National League in runs scored with 612 in eighty-four games and also in team batting average, at a .296 team clip.

A glorious image of the 1874 champion Boston Red Stockings, who featured (top, left to right) Cal McVey, Albert Spalding, Deacon White, Ross Barnes; (bottom, left to right) Jim O'Rourke, Andy Leonard, George Wright, Harry Wright, George Hall, Harry Schafer, and Tommy Beals (NATIONAL BASEBALL LIBRARY, COOPERSTOWN, N.Y.).

Apparently, a fierce rivalry developed that season between George's Providence club and Harry's Boston club. Newspaper accounts from that year reported that Harry's Boston players actually traveled to Providence on an off day to root against George's Grays.[14] Harry's Boston boys later skulked away silently when George's nine defeated the visiting Cincinnati club. At the end of the season, George's Grays beat out Harry's Red Stockings by five games for the National League gonfalon.

In 1880, though, George returned to Boston for two seasons, but finished out his playing career back in Providence in 1882.

George Wright was an all-around sportsman after his baseball days ended. He was the first sporting goods entrepreneur to manufacture tennis equipment in the United States. He also was credited with having played the first game of golf in New England, and possibly in the United States, after he ordered some golf clubs from a distributor in Scotland without knowing exactly what the clubs were supposed to be used for. A Scottish associate visiting Wright in Boston explained the game to him and later sent him a rule book from Scotland, and Wright learned to play the newfangled game.

In 1890 George Wright laid out the first nine-hole golf course in the nation, at Franklin Park in Hyde Park, Massachusetts. He also continued to play cricket at the Longwood Cricket Club in Boston. Wright later served on the commission that settled on Cooperstown as the birthplace of baseball, and in 1912, at age 65, he umpired an exhibition baseball game between the United States and Sweden at the fifth Olympics in Stockholm. The National League awarded George Wright its Number One lifetime pass. In 1919, George, Cal McVey, and Oak Taylor were guests of honor at Redland Field in Cincinnati for the infamous World Series between the Reds and the Chicago White Sox, as the Cincinnati club commemorated the Fiftieth anniversary of the unbeaten 1869 Red Stockings.

In a 1915 *New York Sun* interview, George Wright remembered the early days of the game:

> After all there have not been many changes in playing the national game since it was first started. In the early days the players were out for the fun and exercise. There were no leagues or enclosed parks. A ball, a bat and flannels were all the equipment they had. Masks, gloves, mitts, chest protectors, &c., are all modern inventions.
>
> The baseball of the old times was larger, heavier and more elastic than that now in use. No rule governed the length, weight or sizes of the bats. Any kind of wood could be used in their construction. They were of the same diameter as those used nowadays, but the favorite wood was willow, hence the expression, "Use the willow."
>
> The players did not have gloves to protect their hands, consequently more skill was required to catch the ball, because with the greater weight there was danger of severe injuries unless a hard hit or thrown ball was handled perfectly. It was not an unusual thing for a catcher to have both hands black and blue from the impact of the horsehide sphere.
>
> Baseball is on a higher moral plane than it has ever been before. This can be attributed to the umpires. So long as they are given a full charge of the field the game will remain clean. Baseball has no limits and I expect to see interest in it steadily increase with the years to come.[15]

Cincinnati scribe Harry Ellard said of George Wright. "He covered more ground in his position than any other man in the country, and he and Sweasy made a pair that could not be surpassed. He was as active as a cat, and the way he pounced on a hot daisy-cutter and picked it up, or made a running fly catch, was wonderful."[16]

Albert Spalding added:

> His skill as a batsman, baserunner, and his attractive figure on the field, have never been excelled. I had a good opportunity to judge of George Wright's skill as a player; I pitched against his team several times while he was a member of the Cincinnati team, and I was pitcher for the Rockford Club. I also played along with him in the Boston Club from 1871 to 1875, inclusive. His sunny disposition, athletic figure, curly hair and pearly white teeth, with a good-natured smile always playing around them, no matter how exciting the

game was, together with his extraordinary skill in all departments of the game, made him in my opinion one of the most attractive and picturesque figures in baseball. I consider him one of the best all-around players the game has ever produced.[17]

George Wright spent many afternoons in his sunset years in Boston watching the Red Sox play at Fenway Park and the Braves play at Braves Field. He died in Boston on August 21, 1937, at age 90, just weeks after being inducted into the Baseball Hall of Fame.

Harry Wright

Harry Wright took over the reins of the Boston Red Stockings in 1871 and piloted the club to six pennants, including four straight, between 1872 and 1878.

In 1874, Harry led baseball's first tour back to his birthplace country of England. Harry, his brothers George and Sam, Cal McVey, Andy Leonard, Albert Spalding, and other baseballers sailed to Liverpool, staging matches in that city and also in Sheffield — Harry's birthplace — and Manchester, and in Dublin, Ireland.

George Wright would later write a comical story about the trip that involved his older brother Harry: "The trip was a fortunate one as far as accidents were concerned. Nothing serious occurred except on our arrival at Liverpool, where we were taken from the steamer *Ohio* in a small tug-boat, when upon our nearing the dock, Captain Harry being anxious to be the first to land in old England, made a jump from the tug to the dock, with a satchel in each hand, striking fair upon his feet, but both slipped from under him, as the boards were wet from rain, and he landed in England solid."[18]

On April 28, 1876, the baseball world was shocked and saddened to read in the *Cincinnati Enquirer* the news that Harry Wright was dead.[19] The most shocked of anyone was the very-much-alive Harry Wright. At the time of his supposed demise on April 27, Wright was skippering the Red Stockings in Providence as they dropped an error-filled, 13–8 contest. Everyone had a good laugh over the "news" of Harry's premature demise. Another newspaper commented, "Well, if Harry ain't dead, he ought to be, so that he could fully enjoy all the nice things that have been said about him, otherwise they are wasted. After a man's obituary is published in the *Enquirer*, it is time he ceased to live if he knows anything about the proprieties."

While Harry Wright clearly enjoyed his tenure in Boston, and was eminently successful there, he never forgot his glory days in Cincinnati. Upon hearing the news that Cincinnati would be fielding a National League entry in 1876, Harry wrote to his friend and former teammate Oak Taylor, noting, "I am glad to hear that Cincinnati is re-kindling her zeal in the Noble Game, and hope we shall have some of the old-time enthusiasm to enliven us when we visit [Cincinnati] this season."[20]

Harry lauded the Queen City as being a very livable place: "I can recommend it as a residence most heartily. Good climate, good shooting, good people, glorious times when I was there."[21]

Harry Wright piloted the Boston Red Stockings until 1881. The following season, he signed on to manage the Providence Grays of the National League, and he stayed in Rhode Island for two seasons. In an 1883 interview with the *Detroit Free Press*, Captain Harry expounded on the future of the game of baseball:

> I have no doubt that it will grow in the popular esteem from year to year. Baseball has taken a firm hold of the people. Businessmen seem to regard it as one of the most rational ways to spend a summer afternoon. The man who becomes interested in baseball certainly forgets the cares and worries of business, at least during the progress of the game, and for that reason, if there were no others, the game must continue its firm grip.... [Another] point I would like to emphasize is the great desirability of cultivating the ladies. Interest them in baseball, and its tone will steadily improve.[22]

In 1884, Harry took over the helm in Philadelphia, and spent ten years there before retiring from the game in 1893. In 1890, Wright and his Philadelphia squad traveled to Cincinnati for a series of contests there. It marked Harry's return to the Queen City after a lengthy absence. Few in the crowd recognized Harry as he sat on the Philadelphia bench. "There has been a great change in the captain," the *Cincinnati Enquirer* reported. "The years that have rolled around since he wore the red stockings of the Queen City team have left their mark. Instead of a strong, muscular athlete, in the full prime of his manhood, as Harry was in 1869, [the fans now] see a sedate-looking individual in quiet business attire, whose hair and whiskers are plentifully sprinkled with grey."[23]

Harry Wright worked as a newspaper writer after his playing days ended, and he founded the short-lived Wright & Mahn Sporting Goods Company. He also patented a scorecard and allowed his name to be used for promotional purposes by a turnstile manufacturer. In 1893 he was named the honorary umpire-in-chief of the National League, albeit at an annual salary of $2,000. In 1895 Harry was stricken with pneumonia, which was complicated by a rupture of the pleura. He died in an Atlantic City sanatorium on October 3, 1895, at age 60.

April 13, 1896, was Harry Wright Day throughout all of professional baseball. Proceeds were to be collected in order to establish a monument for

Harry Wright's grave at the West Laurel Hill Cemetery in Philadelphia. The day was cold and rainy across most of the Northeast, however, and few cranks flocked to the ballparks that raw spring afternoon. As a result, only $3,349.79 was raised for the memorial. The following winter the National League, at its annual meeting, pledged additional dollars to erect a fitting monument to the quiet, honorable pioneer and manager of the historic 1869 Cincinnati Red Stockings.[24]

"Every magnate in the country is indebted to this man," the *Reach Guide* eulogized in 1896, "for the establishment of baseball as a business, and every patron for fulfilling him with a systematic recreation. Every player is indebted to him for inaugurating an occupation in which he gains a livelihood, and the country at large for adding one more industry ... to furnish employment."[25]

Harry Wright was elected to the Baseball Hall of Fame in 1953.

Epilogue

The meteoric career of the Cincinnati Red Stockings had wrought a very great change in public sentiment, and in the minds of players as well, regarding professionalism. Genuine lovers of the sport, who admired the game for its real worth as an entertaining pastime and invigorating form of exercise, saw in the triumphs of the Reds the dawn of a new era in Base Ball; for they were forced, nolens volens, to recognize that professionalism had come to stay; that by it the game would be presented in its highest state of perfection; that amateurs, devoting the greater portion of their time to other pursuits, could not hope to compete with those whose business it was to play the game — and play it as a business. Hence public opposition to professional Base Ball melted quickly away. The best players needed no other incentive to make them accept the situation, even gleefully, than was found in their love for the sport, coupled with the prospect of gaining a livelihood in a manner so perfectly in accord with their tastes and inclination.[1]

Albert Spalding, 1911

"Well, well, my boy, those days are gone;
No club will ever shine
Like the one which never knew defeat,
The Reds of Sixty-nine."
— Harry Ellard
(National Baseball Library).

151

Notes

1. Base Ball Before the Red Stockings

1. Harold Seymour, *Baseball: The Early Years* (New York: Oxford University Press, 1960), p. 5.
2. Seymour, *Baseball*, p. 5.
3. Gerald Secor Couzens, *A Baseball Album* (New York: Lippencott & Crowell, 1980), p. 15, quoting Varnum L. Collins, *Princeton* (New York: 1914), p. 207.
4. Couzens, *A Baseball Album*, p. 15, quoting Collins, *Princeton*, p. 208.
5. John Thorn and Pete Palmer (Editors), *Total Baseball: The Ultimate Encyclopedia of Baseball* (New York: HarperPerennial, 1993), p. 8.
6. Couzens, *A Baseball Album*, p. 15, quoting Jennie Holliman, *American Sports, 1785–1835* (Durham, North Carolina: 1931), p. 64.
7. Couzens, *A Baseball Album*, p. 15, quoting Thurlow Weed, *Autobiography* (Boston: 1884), p. 203.
8. Thorn and Palmer, *Total Baseball*, p. 8.
9. Gerald Astor, *The Baseball Hall of Fame 50th Anniversary Book* (New York: Prentice Hall Press, 1988), p. 2.
10. Astor, *The Baseball Hall of Fame 50th Anniversary Book*, p. 2.
11. Seymour, *Baseball*, p. 18.
12. Astor, *The Baseball Hall of Fame 50th Anniversary Book*, pp. 2–4.
13. Thorn and Palmer, *Total Baseball*, p. 9.
14. National Association of Base Ball Players, 1858 Playing Rules.
15. *New York Clipper*, July 17, 1869.
16. Robert Smith, *Baseball* (New York: Simon & Schuster, 1970), p. 14.
17. John Durant, *The Story of Baseball in Words and Pictures* (New York: Hastings House, 1973), p. 18.

2. Professionalism Enters the Game

1. Harold Seymour, *Baseball: The Early Years* (New York: Oxford University Press, 1960), p. 25.
2. *New York Clipper*, October 22, 1859.
3. *New York Clipper*, July 21, 1860.
4. George B. Kirsch, *The Creation of American Team Sports: Baseball and Cricket, 1838–72* (Urbana and Chicago: University of Illinois Press, 1989), p. 235.
5. David Q. Voigt, *American Baseball* (Norman: University of Oklahoma Press, 1966) p. 15.
6. *Ball Player's Chronicle*, August 22, 1867.

7. *Ball Player's Chronicle*, August 22, 1867.

8. *Philadelphia Sunday Mercury*, May 6, 1866.

9. Sam Coombs and Bob West (Editors), *Baseball: America's National Game by Albert Spalding* (San Francisco: Halo Books, 1991), pp. 119–123.

10. Voigt, *American Baseball*, p. 18.

11. Seymour, *Baseball*, p. 48.

12. Vagged, *American Baseball*, p. 18.

13. Seymour, *Baseball*, p. 52.

14. Kirsch, *The Creation of American Team Sports*, p. 2.

15. *Harper's Weekly*, October 26, 1867.

16. *Jersey City Daily Times*, August 9, 1865.

17. *Philadelphia Sunday Mercury*, January 24, 1869.

18. Harry Wright letter to William Hulbert, December 29, 1874, in Harry Wright Correspondence, Albert G. Spalding Collection, New York Public Library.

3. A Quest in the Queen City

1. Charles C. Alexander, *Our Game: An American Baseball History* (New York: Henry Holt, 1991), pp. 18–19.

2. Harold Seymour, "Baseball's First Professional Manager," *Ohio Historical Quarterly* (Volume 64, Number 4, October 1955), pp. 409–410.

3. *Frank Leslie's Illustrated Newspaper*, July 17, 1869.

4. Donald Honig, *The Cincinnati Reds: An Illustrated History* (New York: Simon & Schuster, 1992), p. 18.

5. *Ball Player's Chronicle*, November 14, 1867.

6. *Ball Player's Chronicle*, November 14, 1867.

7. 1858 Knickerbocker Base Ball Club Club Book, Albert G. Spalding Collection, New York Public Library.

8. Harold Seymour, *Baseball: The Early Years* (New York: Oxford University Press, 1960), p. 71.

9. Darryl Brock, "The Wright Way," *Sports Heritage* (March/April 1987), pp. 35–41, 93–94.

10. Harold Seymour, "Baseball's First Professional Manager," *Ohio Historical Quarterly* (Volume 64, Number 4, October 1955), pp. 409–410.

4. Building a Ball Club

1. Harold Seymour, *Baseball: The Early Years* (New York: Oxford University Press, 1960), p. 56.

2. David Q. Voigt, *American Baseball* (Norman: University of Oklahoma Press, 1966), p. 24.

3. Darryl Brock and Greg Rhodes, "Red Stockings in the Red: Financial Tribulations of the First Pro Club," SABR Convention (1995), p.1.

4. Daniel Okrent and Harris Lewine (Editors), *The Ultimate Baseball Book* (Boston: Houghton Mifflin, 1979), p. 12.

5. Harry Wright letter to H. B. Philips, Manager, Hornell Base Ball Association, Hornellsville, NY, March 11, 1878, in Harry Wright Correspondence, Albert G. Spalding Collection, New York Public Library.

6. Harry Wright letter to "Friend Jim," March 19, 1877, in Wright Correspondence.

7. Harry Wright letter to H. H. Baker, March 16, 1878, in Wright Correspondence.

8. *New York Clipper*, January 9, 1869; Voigt, *American Baseball*, p. 26.

9. Seymour, *Baseball*, p. 71.

10. Warren Goldstein, *Playing for Keeps: A History of Early Baseball* (Ithaca: Cornell University Press, 1989), p. 113.

11. Darryl Brock, "The Wright Way," *Sports Heritage* (March/April 1987), pp. 35–41, 93–94.

12. *Spirit of the Times*, November 21, 1868.

13. *Ball Player's Chronicle*, August 18, 1867; July 18, 1867; July 25, 1867.

14. Harvey Frommer, *Primitive Baseball: The First Quarter Century of the National Pastime* (New York: Atheneum, 1988), p. 12.

5. Pros — and Their Cons

1. *New York Times*, April 10, 1869.

2. *New York Times*, April 10, 1869.

3. *New York Times*, April 10, 1869.

4. *New York Times*, April 10, 1869.

5. Harold Seymour, *Baseball: The Early Years* (New York: Oxford University Press, 1960), p. 55.

6. Seymour, *Baseball*, p. 55.

7. Samm Coombs and Bob West (Editors), *Baseball: America's National Game by Albert Spalding* (San Francisco: Halo Books, 1991), pp. 119–123.

8. Seymour, *Baseball*, pp. 55–56.

9. Coombs and West, *Baseball: America's National Game by Albert Spalding*, p. 82.

6. To Be Purely Professional

1. Harry Ellard, *Baseball in Cincinnati: A History* (Cincinnati: Johnson & Hardin, 1907), pp. 138–209; *New York Clipper*, January 9, 1869.

2. Harry Wright letter to Charles Tubbs, December 2, 1874, in Harry Wright Correspondence, Albert G. Spalding Collection, New York Public Library.

7. Throwing Down the Gauntlet of Defiance

1. *Philadelphia Sunday Mercury*, February 7, 1869.

2. Samm Coombs and Bob West (Editors), *Baseball: America's National Game by Albert Spalding* (San Francisco: Halo Books, 1991), p. 82.

3. Harry Ellard, *Baseball in Cincinnati: A History* (Cincinnati: Johnson & Hardin, 1907), pp. 138–209.

4. David Q. Voigt, *America Through Baseball* (Chicago: Nelson-Hall, 1976), p. 38.

5. Darryl Brock, "The Wright Way," *Sports Heritage* (March/April 1987), pp. 35–41, 93–94.

6. Arthur Bartlett, *Baseball and Mr. Spalding: The History and Romance of Baseball* (New York: Farrar, Straus and Young, 1951), p. 110.

7. *Daily Alta California*, September 24, 1869.

8. Kevin Grace, "'Bushel Basket' Charlie Gould of Red Stockings," *SABR Baseball Research Journal* (Cooperstown: Society for American Baseball Research, 1984), pp. 82–84.

9. *New York Clipper*, 1874 PreSeason Guide.

10. *New York Sun*, November 14, 1915.

11. Darryl Brock, "The Wright Way," *Sports Heritage* (March/April 1987), pp. 35–41, 93–94.

12. *New York Sun*, November 14, 1915.

13. Darryl Brock, "The Wright Way," *Sports Heritage* (March/April 1987), pp. 35–41, 93–94.

14. *St. Louis Republican*, June 1, 1875.

15. *St. Louis Clipper*, 1874 PreSeason Guide.

16. *National Baseball Hall of Fame and Museum Yearbook*, 1992.

17. *St. Louis Republican*, June 1, 1875.

18. *New York Clipper*, 1874 PreSeason Guide.

19. Harry Wright letter to Henry Chadwick, January 2, 1875, in Harry Wright Correspondence, Albert G. Spalding Collection, New York Public Library.

20. Daniel Okrent and Steve Wulf, *Baseball Anecdotes* (New York: Oxford University Press, 1989), p. 7.

21. *New York Clipper*, 1874 PreSeason Guide.

22. *Sporting Life*, July 5, 1890.

23. *New York Clipper*, 1874 PreSeason Guide.

24. *Boston Times*, June 4, 1876.

25. Harry Wright letter to Henry Chadwick, January 2, 1875, in Wright Correspondence.

26. *Boston Daily Globe*, May 30, 1883.

27. National Association of Base Ball Players, 1867 Playing Rules.

28. National Association of Base Ball Players, 1867 Playing Rules.

8. A Blazing Scarlett in the Spring

1. *New York Clipper*, January 9, 1869.

2. Robert Smith, *Baseball* (New York: Simon & Schuster, 1970), p. 17.

3. David Q. Voigt, *America through Baseball* (Chicago: Nelson-Hall, 1976), p. 34.

4. Warren Goldstein, *Playing for Keeps: A History of Early Baseball* (Ithaca: Cornell University Press, 1989), p. 109.

5. *Cincinnati Enquirer*, April 18, 1869.

6. *Cincinnati Enquirer*, April 25, 1869.

7. *Cincinnati Enquirer*, May 11, 1869.

8. *Cincinnati Enquirer*, May 11, 1869.

9. *Cincinnati Enquirer*, May 16, 1869.

9. Looking to the East

1. Harold Seymour, *Baseball: The Early Years* (New York: Oxford University Press, 1960), p. 57.
2. Harry Ellard, *Baseball in Cincinnati: A History* (Cincinnati: Johnson & Hardin, 1907), pp. 138–209.
3. Ellard, *Baseball in Cincinnati*, pp. 138–209.

10. The Journey Begins

1. David Q. Voigt, *America through Baseball* (Chicago: Nelson-Hall, 1976), p. 37.
2. Voigt, *America through Baseball*, p. 37.
3. Voigt, *America through Baseball*, p. 38.
4. Voigt, *America through Baseball*, p. 37.
5. Voigt, *America through Baseball*, p. 37.
6. *Springfield Daily Union*, June 10, 1869.
7. *Boston Post*, June 11, 1869.

11. The Gotham Showdown

1. Robert Smith, *Baseball in America* (New York: Holt, Rinehart and Winston, 1961), p. 30.
2. *New York Daily Tribune*, June 15, 1869.
3. *Spirit of the Times*, June 26, 1869.
4. Harry Ellard, *Baseball in Cincinnati: A History* (Cincinnati: Johnson & Hardin, 1907), pp. 138–209.
5. David Q. Voigt, *American Baseball* (Norman: University of Oklahoma Press, 1966), p. 32.
6. *New York Daily Tribune*, June 16, 1869.
7. *New York Daily Tribune*, June 17, 1869.
8. Voight, *American Baseball*, p. 30.
9. *Spirit of the Times*, June 26, 1869.

12. "Oh, How Is This for High?"

1. *Spirit of the Times*, June 19, 1869.
2. Greg Rhodes and John Erardi, *The First Boys of Summer* (Cincinnati: Road West, 1994), p. 34.
3. Harry Ellard, *Baseball in Cincinnati: A History* (Cincinnati: Johnson & Hardin, 1907), pp. 138–209.
4. Rhodes and Erardi, *The First Boys of Summer*, p. 36.
5. Rhodes and Erardi, *The First Boys of Summer*, p. 37.
6. Ellard, *Baseball in Cincinnati*, pp. 138–209.
7. Ellard, *Baseball in Cincinnati*, pp. 138–209.
8. Harvey Frommer, *Primitive Baseball: The First Quarter Century of the National Pastime* (New York: Atheneum, 1988), p. 14.

9. Ellard, *Baseball in Cincinnati*, pp. 138–209.

10. Darryl Brock and Greg Rhodes, "Red Stockings in the Red: Financial Tribulations of the First Pro Club," SABR Convention (1995), p. 2.

13. The Glory of the Queen City

1. *Cincinnati Commercial*, July 1, 2, 3, 1869.
2. *Cincinnati Commercial*, July 1, 2, 3, 1869.
3. Gerald Secor Couzens, *A Baseball Album* (New York: Lippincott & Crowell, 1980), p. 1.
4. *Cincinnati Commercial*, July 1, 2, 3, 1869.
5. *Cincinnati Commercial*, July 1, 2, 3, 1869.
6. *Cincinnati Commercial*, July 1, 2, 3, 1869.
7. *Cincinnati Gazette*, July 1, 2, 1869.
8. *Cincinnati Commercial*, July 1, 2, 1869.

14. Unblemished Still

1. Greg Rhodes and John Erardi, *The First Boys of Summer* (Cincinnati: Road West, 1994), p. 51.
2. *Winnebago County Chief*, August 10, 1869.
3. Mark Alvarez (Editor), *The Perfect Game* (Dallas: Taylor, 1993), p. 94.
4. Alvarez, *The Perfect Game*, p. 94.
5. Alvarez, *The Perfect Game*, p. 94.

15. "A Most Contemptible Trick"

1. *Cincinnati Commercial*, August 27, 1869; Harry Ellard, *Baseball in Cincinnati: A History* (Cincinnati: Johnson & Hardin, 1907), pp. 138–209.
2. Damon Rice, *Seasons Past: The Story of Baseball's First Century as Witnessed by Three Generations of an American Family* (New York: Praeger, 1976), p. 18.
3. Rice, *Seasons Past*, p. 18.
4. Rice, *Seasons Past*, p. 18.
5. Rice, *Seasons Past*, p. 19.
6. Rice, *Seasons Past*, p. 19.
7. Rice, *Seasons Past*, p. 20.
8. Ellard, *Baseball in Cincinnati*, pp. 166–169.
9. *Cincinnati Gazette*, August 27, 1869.
10. Ellard, *Baseball in Cincinnati*, pp. 138–209.

16. 103 to 81

1. Cincinnati Red Stockings Scorebooks, 1868–1870, Albert G. Spalding Collection, New York Public Library.

17. The California Tour

1. Harold Rosenthal, *The 10 Best Years of Baseball* (Chicago: Contemporary Books, 1979), p. 87.

2. Harold Seymour, *Baseball: The Early Years* (New York: Oxford University Press, 1960), p. 202.

3. Greg Rhodes and John Erardi, *The First Boys of Summer* (Cincinnati: Road West, 1994), p. 67.

4. *St. Louis Democrat*, September 16, 1869.

5. Rhodes and Erardi, *The First Boys of Summer*, p. 68.

6. David Cataneo, *Peanuts and Crackerjack: A Treasury of Baseball Legends and Lore* (Nashville: Rutledge Hill Press, 1991), p. 62.

7. *Daily Alta California*, September 24, 1869.

8. *San Francisco Chronicle*, September 25, 1869.

9. *Daily Alta California*, September 23, 1869.

10. *San Francisco Chronicle*, September 28, 1869.

11. *Daily Alta California*, September 26, 1869.

12. *Daily Alta California*, September 26, 1869.

13. Darryl Brock, "The Wright Way," *Sports Heritage* (March/April 1987), pp. 35–41, 93–94.

14. *Daily Alta California*, September 26, 1869.

15. *Daily Alta California*, September 26, 1869.

16. *Daily Alta California*, September 28, 1869.

17. *Daily Alta California*, September 29, 1869.

18. *Daily Alta California*, September 30, 1869.

19. *Daily Alta California*, October 1, 1869.

20. *San Francisco Chronicle*, October 2, 1869.

21. *San Francisco Chronicle*, October 2, 1869.

22. *Daily Alta California*, October 3, 1869.

23. *Daily Alta California*, October 3, 1869.

24. Harry Wright letter to Charles Neal, January 8, 1879, in Harry Wright Correspondence, Albert G. Spalding Collection, New York Public Library.

25. Rhodes and Erardi, *The First Boys of Summer*, pp. 72–73.

26. Rhodes and Erardi, *The First Boys of Summer*, p. 73.

27. Darryl Brock and Greg Rhodes, "Red Stockings in the Red: Financial Tribulations of the First Pro Club," SABR Convention, (1995), p. 2.

18. "Veni! Vidi!! Vici!!!"

1. Cincinnati Red Stockings Scorebooks, 1868–1870, Albert G. Spalding Collection, New York Public Library.

2. Mark Alvarez (Editor), *The Perfect Game* (Dallas: Taylor Publishing Co., 1993), pp. 89–94.

3. Alvarez, *The Perfect Game*, pp. 89–94.

4. Alvarez, *The Perfect Game*, pp. 89–94.

5. Harry Ellard, *Baseball in Cincinnati: A History* (Cincinnati: Johnson & Hardin, 1907), pp. 138–209.

6. Greg Rhodes and John Erardi, *The First Boys of Summer* (Cincinnati: Road West Publishing Company, 1994), p. 82.

7. Rhodes and Erardi, *The First Boys of Summer*, p. 82.

8. Samm Coombs and Bob West (Editors), *Baseball: America's National Game by Albert Spalding* (San Francisco: Halo Books, 1991), pp. 83–85.

19. 1870: Improving on Perfection

1. *New York Sun*, November 14, 1915.

2. Harry Ellard, *Baseball in Cincinnati: A History* (Cincinnati: Johnson & Hardin, 1907), pp. 138–209.

3. Greg Rhodes and John Erardi, *The First Boys of Summer* (Cincinnati: Road West Publishing Company, 1994), p. 83.

4. *New York Times*, April 7, 1870.

5. *New York Times*, April 7, 1870.

6. *New York Clipper*, October 30, 1869.

7. Harvey Frommer, *Primitive Baseball: The First Quarter Century of the National Pastime* (New York: Atheneum, 1988), pp. 15–16.

8. Cited in *Philadelphia Sunday Mercury*, December 5, 1869.

9. Ellard, *Baseball in Cincinnati*, pp. 138–209.

10. Cincinnati Red Stockings Scorebooks, 1868–1870, Albert G. Spalding Collection, New York Public Library and Rhodes and Erardi, *The First Boys of Summer*, p. 87.

11. Rhodes and Erardi, *The First Boys of Summer*, p. 88.

12. Rhodes and Erardi, *The First Boys of Summer*, p. 94.

20. The Battle of Brooklyn: "Though Beaten, Not Disgraced"

1. *New York Daily Tribune*, June 14, 1870.

2. George Bulkley, "The Day the Reds Lost," *The National Pastime* (Cooperstown: Society for American Baseball Research, 1983), pp. 5–9.

3. Bulkley, "The Day the Reds Lost," p. 6.

4. Bulkley, "The Day the Reds Lost," p. 7.

5. Daniel Okrent and Steve Wulf, *Baseball Anecdotes* (New York: Oxford University Press, 1989), p. 10.

6. Okrent and Wulf, *Baseball Anecdotes*, p. 10.

7. Bulkley, "The Day the Reds Lost," p. 7.

8. Bulkley, "The Day the Reds Lost," p. 8.

9. *New York Daily Tribune*, June 15, 1870.

10. Bulkley, "The Day the Reds Lost," p. 8.

11. Okrent and Wulf, *Baseball Anecdotes*, p. 9.

12. Bulkley, "The Day the Reds Lost," p. 9; Richard Goldstein, *Superstars and Screwballs: 100 Years of Brooklyn Baseball* (New York: Dutton, 1991), p. 22.

13. Harold Seymour, *Baseball: The Early Years* (New York: Oxford University Press, 1960), p. 57.

14. Harry Ellard, *Baseball in Cincinnati: A History* (Cincinnati: Johnson & Hardin, 1907), pp. 138–209.

15. *New York Daily Tribune*, June 15, 1870.

16. *New York Daily Herald*, June 15, 1870.

17. *New York Daily Tribune*, June 15, 1870.

18. Greg Rhodes and John Erardi, *The First Boys of Summer* (Cincinnati: Road West, 1994), p. 99.

19. Ellard, *Baseball in Cincinnati*, pp. 190–195.

21. The Face of Mortality

1. *New York Daily Tribune*, June 19, 1870.

2. Gerald Secor Couzens, *A Baseball Album* (New York: Lippincott & Crowell, 1980), pp. 63–65, quoting William Arthur Cummings, "How I Pitched the First Curve," *Baseball Magazine*, 1908.

3. Greg Rhodes and John Erardi, *The First Boys of Summer* (Cincinnati: Road West, 1994), p. 106.

4. Cincinnati Red Stockings Scorebooks, 1868–1870, Albert G. Spalding Collection, New York Public Library.

5. Rhodes and Erardi, *The First Boys of Summer*, pp. 107–109.

22. After the Ball

1. Harry Ellard, *Baseball in Cincinnati: A History* (Cincinnati: Johnson & Hardin, 1907), pp. 138–209.

2. Warren Goldstein, *Playing for Keeps: A History of Early Baseball* (Ithaca: Cornell University Press, 1989), p. 117.

3. Ellard, *Baseball in Cincinnati*, pp. 138–209.

4. Greg Rhodes and John Erardi, *The First Boys of Summer* (Cincinnati: Road West, 1994), p. 118.

5. Ellard, *Baseball in Cincinnati*, pp. 138–209.

23. "Not a Porkopolian Has Heart Enough Left to Tell of the Defeat"

1. Greg Rhodes and John Erardi, *The First Boys of Summer* (Cincinnati: Road West, 1994), p. 121.

2. *Cincinnati Gazette*, September 8, 1870.

3. *Cincinnati Gazette*, September 8, 1870.

4. Rhodes and Erardi, *The First Boys of Summer*, p. 122.

5. *Chicago Tribune*, September 8, 10, 1870.

6. Rhodes and Erardi, *The First Boys of Summer*, p. 124.

7. *Chicago Tribune*, September 8, 10, 1870.

24. The Dye in the Stockings Begins to Fade

1. Greg Rhodes and John Erardi, *The First Boys of Summer* (Cincinnati: Road West, 1994), p. 124.

2. Rhodes and Erardi, *The First Boys of Summer*, p. 126.

3. Cincinnati Red Stockings Scorebooks, 1868–1870, Albert G. Spalding Collection, New York Public Library.

4. Rhodes and Erardi, *The First Boys of Summer*, p. 130.

25. *The Death of a Baseball Club*

1. Cincinnati Red Stockings Scorebooks, 1868–1870, Albert G. Spalding Collection, New York Public Library.
2. *New York Sun*, October 15, 1911.
3. *New York Clipper*, August 27, 1870.
4. *Cincinnati Commercial*, October 29, 1870.
5. Harold Seymour, *Baseball: The Early Years* (New York: Oxford University Press, 1960), p. 59.
6. Greg Rhodes and John Erardi, *The First Boys of Summer* (Cincinnati: Road West, 1994), p. 133.
7. *New York Times*, November 27, 1870.
8. Harry Ellard, *Baseball in Cincinnati: A History* (Cincinnati: Johnson & Hardin, 1907), pp. 138–209.

26. *A New League, a New City*

1. Cited in *Spirit of the Times*, November 26, 1870.
2. Samm Coombs and Bob West (Editors), *Baseball: America's National Game by Albert Spalding* (San Francisco: Halo Books, 1991), pp. 93.
3. Harvey Frommer, *Primitive Baseball: The First Quarter Century of the National Pastime* (New York: Atheneum, 1988), p. 17.
4. John Thorn and Pete Palmer (Editors), *Total Baseball: The Ultimate Encyclopedia of Baseball* (New York: HarperPerennial, 1993), p. 10.
5. Donald Honig, *The Cincinnati Reds: An Illustrated History* (New York: Simon & Schuster, 1992), p. 205.
6. Jack Selzer, *Baseball in the Nineteenth Century: An Overview* (Cooperstown: Society for American Baseball Research, 1986), p. 9.

27. *"A Remarkable Band of Ball Players"*

1. Harry Ellard, *Baseball in Cincinnati: A History* (Cincinnati: Johnson & Hardin, 1907), p. 175.
2. Harry Wright letter to Charles Hadel, May 2, 1874, in Harry Wright Correspondence, Albert G. Spalding Collection, New York Public Library.
3. Robert Tiemann and Mark Rucker (Editors), *Nineteenth Century Stars* (Kansas City: Society for American Baseball Research, 1989), p 17.
4. Asa Brainard letter to Harry Wright, October 12, 1882, in Wright Correspondence.
5. Asa Brainard letter to Harry Wright, December 10, 1882, in Wright Correspondence.
6. Asa Brainard letter to Harry Wright, December 10, 1882, in Wright Correspondence.
7. Tiemann and Rucker, *Nineteenth Century Stars*, p. 17.
8. Kevin Grace, "'Bushel Basket' Charlie Gould of Red Stockings," *SABR Baseball Research Journal* (Cooperstown: Society for American Baseball Research, 1984), p. 84.

9. Harry Wright letter to Charles Hadel, April 8, 1874, in Wright Correspondence.

10. Tiemann and Rucker, *Nineteenth Century Stars*, p. 77.

11. *Sporting Life*, June 23, 1906.

12. Doug Allison letter, January 20, 1914.

13. Tiemann and Rucker, *Nineteenth Century Stars*, p. 92.

14. Darryl Brock, "The Wright Way," *Sports Heritage* (March/April 1987), pp. 35–41, 93–94.

15. *New York Sun*, November 14, 1915.

16. Ellard, *Baseball in Cincinnati*, pp. 138–209.

17. Ellard, *Baseball in Cincinnati*, pp. 175–176.

18. George Wright, *George Wright's Book for 1875* (Boston, 1875), p. 24.

19. *Cincinnati Enquirer*, April 28, 1876.

20. Harry Wright letter to O. P. Taylor, April 16, 1877, in Wright Correspondence.

21. Harry Wright letter, January 5, 1878, in Wright Correspondence.

22. *Detroit Free Press*, 1883, cited in Albert G. Spalding Scrapbooks, Albert G. Spalding Collection, New York Public Library.

23. *Cincinnati Enquirer*, September 27, 1890.

24. Lee Allen, *100 Years of Baseball* (New York: Bartholomew House, 1950), p. 21.

25. Harvey Frommer, *Primitive Baseball: The First Quarter Century of the National Pastime* (New York: Atheneum, 1988), pp. 95–96.

Epilogue

1. Samm Coombs and Bob West (Editors), *Baseball: America's National Game by Albert Spalding* (San Francisco: Halo Books, 1991), pp. 95–96.

Bibliography

Books

Alexander, Charles C. *Our Game: An American Baseball History.* New York: Henry Holt & Co., 1991.

Allen, Lee. *The Cincinnati Reds.* New York: Putnam, 1948.

_____. *100 Years of Baseball.* New York: Bartholomew House, 1950.

Alvarez, Mark (Editor). *The Perfect Game.* Dallas: Taylor, 1993.

Astor, Gerald. *The Baseball Hall of Fame 50th Anniversary Book.* New York: Prentice Hall Press, 1988.

Bartlett, Arthur. *Baseball and Mr. Spalding: The History and Romance of Baseball.* New York: Farrar, Straus and Young, 1951.

Brock, Darryl. *If I Never Get Back.* New York: Ballantine Books, 1989, 1991.

Cataneo, David. *Peanuts and Crackerjack: A Treasury of Baseball Legends and Lore.* Nashville: Rutledge Hill Press, 1991.

Coffin, Tristram Potter. *The Illustrated Book of Baseball Folklore.* New York: The Seabury Press, 1975.

Coombs, Samm, and Bob West (Editors). *Baseball: America's National Game by Albert Spalding.* San Francisco: Halo Books, 1991.

Couzens, Gerald Secor. *A Baseball Album.* New York: Lippincott & Crowell, 1980.

Durant, John. *The Story of Baseball in Words and Pictures.* New York: Hastings House, 1973.

Ellard, Harry. *Baseball in Cincinnati: A History.* Cincinnati: Johnson & Hardin, 1907.

Frommer, Harvey. *Primitive Baseball: The First Quarter Century of the National Pastime.* New York: Atheneum, 1988.

Goldstein, Richard. *Superstars and Screwballs: 100 Years of Brooklyn Baseball.* New York: Dutton, 1991.

Goldstein, Warren. *Playing for Keeps: A History of Early Baseball.* Ithaca: Cornell University Press, 1989.

Honig, Donald. *The Cincinnati Reds: An Illustrated History.* New York: Simon & Schuster, 1992.

Kirsch, George B. *The Creation of American Team Sports: Baseball and Cricket, 1838–1872.* Urbana and Chicago: University of Illinois Press, 1989.

Okrent, Daniel, and Harris Lewine (Editors). *The Ultimate Baseball Book.* Boston: Houghton Mifflin, 1979.

Okrent, Daniel, and Steve Wulf. *Baseball Anecdotes.* New York: Oxford University Press, 1989.

Orem, Preston D. *Baseball 1845–1881.* Altadena: Preston D. Orem, 1961.

Reichler, Joseph L. (Editor). *The Baseball Encyclopedia: The Complete and Official Record of Major League Baseball.* New York: MacMillan, 1982.

Rhodes, Greg, and John Erardi. *The First Boys of Summer.* Cincinnati: Road West, 1994.

Rice, Damon. *Seasons Past: The Story of Baseball's First Century as Witnessed by Three Generations of an American Family.* New York: Praeger, 1976.

Rosenburg, John M. *The Story of Baseball.* New York: Random House, 1964.

Rosenthal, Harold. *The 10 Best Years of Baseball.* Chicago: Contemporary Books, 1979.

Selzer, Jack. *Baseball in the Nineteenth Century: An Overview.* Cooperstown: Society for American Baseball Research, 1986.

Seymour, Harold. *Baseball: The Early Years.* New York: Oxford University Press, 1960.

Smith, Ken. *Baseball's Hall of Fame.* New York: Grosset & Dunlap, 1970.

Smith, Robert. *Baseball.* New York: Simon & Schuster, 1970.

_____. *Baseball in America.* New York: Holt, Rinehart and Winston, 1961.

Thorn, John, and Pete Palmer (Editors). *Total Baseball: The Ultimate Encyclopedia of Baseball.* New York: HarperPerrenial, 1993.

Tiemann, Robert and Mark Rucker (Editors). *Nineteenth Century Stars.* Kansas City: Society for American Baseball Research, 1989.

Urdang, Laurence (Editor). *The Timetables of American History.* New York: Simon & Schuster, 1981.

Voigt, David Q. *American Baseball.* Norman: University of Oklahoma Press, 1966.

_____. *America through Baseball.* Chicago: Nelson-Hall, 1976.

Walker, Robert Harris. *Cincinnati and the Big Red Machine.* Bloomington and Indianapolis: University of Indiana Press, 1988.

Wright, George. *George Wright's Book for 1875.* Boston: 1875.

Newspapers

Boston Daily Globe, 1883.
Boston Herald, 1870–73.
Boston Post, 1869–75.
Boston Times, 1875–76.
Chicago Post, 1870.
Chicago Times, 1870.
Chicago Tribune, 1870–76.
Cincinnati Commercial, 1868–70.
Cincinnati Enquirer, 1869–76, 1890.
Cincinnati Gazette, 1869–70.
Cincinnati Times, 1869–70.
Daily Alta California, 1869.
Day Book, 1869.
Dayton Herald, 1870.
Detroit Free Press, 1883.
Frank Leslie's Illustrated Newspaper, 1869.

Jersey City Daily Times, 1865.
New York Daily Tribune, 1869–70.
New York Herald, 1870.
New York Sun, 1870, 1911, 1915.
New York Times, 1868–72.
New York World, 1870.
Paterson Press, 1867.
Philadelphia Sunday Mercury, 1866–71.
San Francisco Chronicle, 1869.
Springfield Daily Union, 1869.
St. Louis Democrat, 1869.
St. Louis Republican, 1875.
Washington Evening Star, 1867.
Washington Republican, 1869.
Winnebago County Chief, 1869.
Worcester Evening Gazette, 1870.

Journals, Guides and Magazines

Ball Player's Chronicle, 1867.
Baseball Magazine, 1908.
Baseball Research Journal, 1984.
Harper's Weekly, 1866–70.
Ohio Historical Quarterly, 1955.
National Baseball Hall of Fame and Museum Yearbook, 1992.

New England Base Ballist, 1867.
Reach's Official Base Ball Guide, 1896.
Spirit of the Times, 1868–70.
Sporting Life, 1890, 1904, 1906.
Sports Heritage, 1987.
The National Pastime, 1983–84, 1992.

Scorebooks

Wright, Harry. Cincinnati Red Stockings Scorebooks, 1868–70, from the Albert G. Spalding Collection of Harry Wright Scorebooks, Rare Books and Manuscripts Division, The New York Public Library, Astor, Lenox and Tilden Foundations.

Correspondence

Wright, Harry. Harry Wright Correspondence, 1871–1885, Vols. 1, 3, 4, and 6, from the Albert G. Spalding Collection of Harry Wright Correspondence, Rare Books and Manuscripts Division, The New York Public Library, Astor, Lenox and Tilden Foundations.

Scrapbooks

Spalding, Albert G. Albert G. Spalding Scrapbooks, Vols. 1, 2, 4, 5, 7–12, from the Albert G. Spalding Collection of Albert G. Spalding Scrapbooks, Rare Books and Manuscripts Division, The New York Public Library, Astor, Lenox and Tilden Foundations.

Club Books

Knickerbocker Base Ball Club. Knickerbocker Base Ball Club Club Books, 1854–1868, from the Albert G. Spalding Collection of Knickerbocker Base Ball Club Club Books, Rare Books and Manuscripts Division, The New York Public Library, Astor, Lenox and Tilden Foundations.

Papers

Brock, Darryl, and Greg Rhodes. "Red Stockings in the Red: Financial Tribulations of the First Pro Club," SABR Convention 1995.

Index